D1084113

Morning Sidekick
Journal

Volume 1 of 3

Conquer Your Mornings, Conquer Your Life.

Created with love by
Amir Atighehchi, Ari Banayan, & Mikey Ahdoot

For information about permission to reproduce elections from this book, email team@habitnest.com
Visit our website at www.HabitNest.com

PUBLISHER'S DISCLAIMER

While the publisher and author have used their best efforts in preparing this book, they make no representations or warranties with respect to the accuracy or completeness of the contents of this book. The advice and strategies contained herein may not be suitable for your situation. You should consult with a professional where appropriate. Neither the publisher nor the author shall be liable for any loss of profit or any other commercial damages, including but not limited to special, incidental, consequential, or other damages.

The company, product, and service names used in this book are for identification purposes only. All trademarks and registered trademarks are the property of their respective owners.

SPECIAL THANKS

We'd like to extend a wholehearted, sincere thank you to Skyler Wolpert and Lindsay McDermott for formatting + editing help. We love ya!

ISBN (Sunrise Red): 9780692726716

SEVENTH EDITION

The Habit Nest Mission

We are a team of people **obsessed with taking ACTION** and **learning new things** as quickly as possible.

We love finding the **fastest, most effective ways** to build a new skill, then **systemizing that process for others**.

With building new habits, we empathize with others every step of the way *because we go through the same process ourselves*. We live and breathe everything in our company.

We use our hard-earned intuition to outline **beautifully designed, intuitive products** to help people live **happier, more fulfilled lives**.

Everything we create comes with a mix of **bite-sized information, strategy, and accountability**. This hands you a simple yet **drastically effective roadmap** to build **any skill** or habit with.

We take this a step further by diving into **published scientific studies,** the opinions of subject-matter **experts,** and the **feedback we get from customers** to further enhance all the products we create.

Ultimately, Habit Nest is a **practical, action-oriented startup** aimed at helping others take back decisional authority over every action they take. We're here to help people live **wholesome, rewarding lives** at the **brink of their potential!**

– Amir Atighehchi, Ari Banayan, & Mikey Ahdoot
Cofounders of Habit Nest

Table of Contents

Our Mission for This Journal

The truth of the matter is most people need some form of guidance when it comes to personal development.

Because you bought this journal, you're probably someone who is generally into personal development. You're probably familiar with ordinary journals that promise to help you remain productive, create useful routines, etc.

Let's be real.

This journal is a compilation of the best tips and strategies discovered by people who have truly mastered their mornings. We've dug through many 300-page books, podcasts, scientific studies behind willpower, cool products/apps/gadgets, and dissected successful leaders' strategies to find the golden nuggets of info and present them here.

The result is a journal bringing something new to the table. **Actionable tips** and **motivating content** are what we're all about.

Every day, for 66 days, we're going to give you the information, motivation, and accountability you need to stay consistent in making significant strides towards your goal of bettering yourself.

Why 66 days? In a recent study on human behavior, researcher Phillippa Lally discovered that on average, it takes 66 days to form a habit. In reality, there is no exact, definite, magical moment. But from personal experience, 66 days is a long enough time to build the habit so strongly that you can tap into it at any future point in your life.

You are building a life-altering habit here that you can use at any moment in your future. The beauty about this is by diving head first into mastering your mornings, you'll immediately start seeing the benefits on day ONE.

Our mission is to be your book-sized personal trainer for building this life-altering habit into your day to day life.

The way you start your morning sets the tone for the rest of your day. Building a morning routine that sets you up for the perfect day is one of the big 'secrets' everyone knows, but for some reason, can't pull off.

Throughout this journey, it's common to have internal dialogue saying things like "I'm not a morning person... I sleep too late... Just 5 more minutes..."

Remember:
Excuses are the *enemy of success*. Excuses are the *enemy of change*. Excuses are the *enemy of your goals*. Today we stop making excuses, together.

In this moment, you're already doing something amazing. The fact that you're reading this means somewhere in you there is a burning desire to really add this habit and make it stick.

Let's make it stick and add value to our lives in an amazing, indescribable way.

The 'Why'

1

Understanding Your Why

As humans, what sets us apart from other animals is our desire to be great as opposed to simply survive. We all have a vision of what our ideal life might look like.

The absolute most important aspect of changing your life for the better is… **Establishing your clear, unwavering purpose (your *Why*).**

The thing is, when we forget (and we forget quite often) the reason we're struggling to improve our lives, we tend to retreat to our habitual selves - to the person we were before we made the decision to change.

Having a clear understanding of your 'why' (what you want to change and why you want to change it) is what pulls you through the tough times you will inevitably face when altering your habits.

Here are a few simple questions that **you should take your time to answer sincerely before moving on**.

These questions are aimed at getting to the root of what drives you, at what gets you up every single morning.

The point of this is to guide you to make concrete decisions about how to set up your morning to fit the beautiful vision you have for your perfect life.

If you're going to even make an attempt at this, you better know why you're doing it in the first place.

Seriously. Take the time to define your dream life.

1. What would my life look like if I did a morning routine filled with incredible habits every single day for the next 30 days?

    Order and Structure.
    A productive and meaningful day.

2. What sort of ripple effect would doing a morning routine have on other areas of my life? On other people's lives around me?

    It would strengthen my body, mind,
    emotions and spirit.

It would make me feel better about myself.

3. What would my life look like if I did not do this? What would I be missing out on? How would missing those make me feel?

It would be disorderly. Every morning would be wasted not doing anything productive and just being sedentary, watching TV, scrolling through social media. This would make me feel worse about myself, not having drive or being productive or having purpose

4. What life goals do I consistently avoid making time for? Can I implement taking action on these goals into my morning routine?

Reading more, I could be taking the time I have in the morning to do some light reading to activate my mind and expand my knowledge

---

Bonus Question: What are the top hurdles I'm facing with getting to bed on time / mastering my mornings? What do I need to do to overcome these?

Working to late in the day.
Being easily distracted in entertainment.
Not having a bedtime routine to follow.
Snoozing too much in the morning from lack of sleep

Bookmark this section and flip back here the next time you're struggling to stay consistent with this habit.

This section is your SOS Lifeline.

The 'Who'

The Three Factors of Behavior Change

James Clear, author of *Atomic Habits*, writes that there are essentially three parts to behavior change (we love your work, James!).

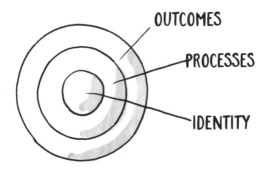

1. The Outcomes

The first is the outside layer: The Outcomes. This is synonymous with your goals (e.g. waking up at XX time every day, Monday through Friday).

Outcomes are most useful at setting a larger, over-arching vision for where you want to go. The downsides of over-focusing on your outcomes are relying on hitting your goals to bring you happiness instead of enjoying the process, and a lack of practicality for what to do day-to-day.

Your outcomes are likely to change over the course of your life to match your ever-evolving goals and needs.

2. The Processes

The second, middle layer, is about processes — this boils down to what system and action steps you put in place to allow your outcomes to come to fruition. These are things like *I will go to bed with my phone in airplane mode and not turn it back on/ Set 3 alarms at my designated wake-up time/ Do whatever it takes to not snooze.* Processes are synonymous with strategies and tactics.

These can be very useful, especially when you find one that clicks, and you'll see a number for you to experiment with sprinkled throughout this journal.

These processes are likely to change over time as you test them out. See what works best for you and switch things up when you get bored / desensitized to them.

3a. Your Identity

This one's the big kahuna. This is the inner-most layer, matching who your internal belief is of yourself as a person. The biggest mistake people make in enacting behavior change is placing way too large of a focus on the first two parts of this puzzle, while entirely forgetting about the third and the most impactful — how you view yourself.

By properly emphasizing WHO you want to grow into, you will maximize your self-respect, satisfaction, and ability to control your actions — more than any motivation or strategy can give you. Your identity is what you can always fall back on to set your intuition, to guide you to what you should really be doing.

An example of setting your identity is:

"I'm someone who can wake up anytime I want and make the most of every morning of my life."

*After defining the identity you want to grow into for yourself, chances are this will **not change much**, but rather, only **strengthen over time** based on your actions.*

3b. Your Identity on Your Off-Days

As much as this plays a role in building towards your goals, it's equally as important in regards to times where you fall off the wagon.

Most people subconsciously forget about what their self-identity looks like when this happens, allowing a massive negative self-view to kick in.

This leads to a major emotional factor, *guilt*, to kick in, and as many studies have shown, **guilt is a willpower destroyer** (these studies are cited at the end of the book).

Instead, mindfully set your identity in these situations…

Grow into the person who uses every opportunity of falling off-track to further strengthen your ability to *switch from your off-days back to being on-track.*

Chances are, you won't do a morning routine, every single day, for the rest of your life, right? Life is about knowing which habits to employ, at the right time, to help you get the most fulfillment out of life.

This involves testing different things and seeing how they serve your life's purpose. In order to really do this, you must master the ability to switch back and forth and discover how to quickly rebuild the momentum you had with your habits, without any guilt that you "lost your mojo."

Be the type of person who can forgive yourself for your mistakes, who will love yourself unconditionally, and be a true best friend to yourself (because if you can't, who will?).

We know these are big emphases on emotional states that can come off as "fluffy," but the truth is our fulfillment in life is directly tied to our emotional states. Learning how to master them is the true feat of this journal, not just building up a specific habit.

Establishing Your Identity

Write your identity statements below.

What kind of person do you want to grow into through this process?

Someone who can conquor anything they put their mind to, follow through with it confidently.

What kind of person do you want to be when you fall off the wagon of your habits? What do you want to remember about who you are and how you can repurpose these days to serve your life?

Stay strong, remember the bigger picture, don't sweat the small stuff and let it demotivate you. Remember what you're trying to accomplish and get back on track.

The 'What'

Phases of Building a New Habit

The development of building a habit happens in stages. There's science behind all kinds of different theories about the stages that come along with altering habits. Here's what we found is the most accurate.

*Days 1-7, **Hell Week.***

…This is going to suck.
It's going to suck because you're rewiring a lifetime habit to be totally different. Expect HELL. You're going to wake up EXHAUSTED. You will NOT easily fall asleep, especially on nights 1 and 2.

This will all fade. Guaranteed. It will fade because you will train your body to jump out of bed when you need to wake up. You will train it to turn off the lights at a specific time & shut off notifications, no matter how hyper your brain is. It will be tough, though your brain will learn. Your body will learn.

But for your brain and body to adapt, you must take action. You must distrust the challenging thoughts your brain will naturally give and show it what you want it to adapt to.

Daily challenge prompts in the journal will give you specific actions to stay focused on while affirmations will set the tone for the direction your life is headed in.

Days 8-21, Staying Consistent.

The good news is that after you've gotten through the first week, the process is a lot easier. You've now hopefully figured out a few approaches that work. Your brain is beginning to understand the changes you're making and the fact that the morning time is extremely useful. Your body is slowly growing accustomed to your new hours. You're seeing the benefits of getting up and starting your day with intention.

During this period, a kick of inspiration can make all the difference. Developing habits takes time and just because you've surpassed the most difficult phase doesn't mean you're off the hook. You'll be reading stories of successful people and their morning routines, getting daily challenges to keep you motivated, and learning some more expert strategies along the way to keep the learning process going.

Days 22 - 66, Hardwiring - Retaining Interest in Your Personal Improvement.

Once you've passed phase 2, you know for a fact that YOU CAN DO THIS. It's amazing. All it takes is just about a month to add the habit, but that doesn't mean that phase 3 isn't crucial, because it is.

To build a habit means to become mechanical in a certain way. Your mind and your body will be used to the morning hours, you'll know the benefits of having a morning routine, but you still need to reach the point where there's no thinking about it anymore.

During Phase 3 you'll get really cool and interesting tools that you might find useful for mastering your mornings. We'll continue to provide you with stories of successful people for motivation, and we'll continue to sprinkle in affirmations along the way to keep your brain active in making your morning routine a part of your DNA.

Days 66 and on, Habit Mastery.

At this point you've built up the muscle memory for mastering your mornings that you can use for life. Even if you won't be waking up early and doing a morning routine every day — after building this skill once, you'll be able to pick it back up at any future point easily.

From here, tweaking and experimenting with your mornings is what it's all about. Try different habits. Try different orders. Test out different wake-up and go-to-bed times. You'll eventually find a rhythm that works well. The best part is you'll be navigating this like a pro at this point.

Experimenting can be interesting and enlightening. Feel free to plug in new habits you want to add to your life - the mornings are an incredible time to do them.

The Daily Content

Every single piece of content you're getting is a product of countless hours of sweat and research done by our team to ensure we're doing our best to:

1. Light a fire in you to succeed in adding the habit.
2. Provide you with the necessary knowledge and information to make mastering your mornings simple and easy.
3. Make adding the habit fun and interesting.

Not only is every individual piece of content chosen amongst thousands of competing options, but as mentioned in the previous section, the order of the content has been creatively designed to get you through the struggles associated with the different stages of adding habits.

DAY 1   DAY 2   DAY 3   DAY 4   DAY 5

PRO-TIP 1   PRO-TIP 2   SUCCESS STORY   DAILY CHALLENGE 1   DAILY CHALLENGE 2

Here are the different types of content you can expect:

Pro-Tips

Pro-tips are the golden little nuggets of information you get to make implementing the habit on a day-to-day basis as simple and painless as possible. The point is to give you expert tips and hacks to get you going, and the variety and diversity of the different pro-tips will provide you with countless options for how to succeed in adding the habit.

Daily Challenges

The daily challenge prompts you'll be receiving will be immensely important to your success in becoming a morning riser.

Why?

They each help target a different area of discipline that will guide you in forcing yourself to do what's right, especially when you *don't feel like it.*

By strengthening this willpower muscle inside you using small, very specific daily challenges, your self-discipline will grow more and more every single day. These daily challenges apply not just to conquering your mornings, but to all other aspects of your life — from curbing negative habits and distractions to building other healthy habits as well.

Clips & Podcasts

There's nothing as motivating as simultaneously seeing the passion in someone's eyes, hearing the truth in someone's voice, and feeling the intensity of their struggle. Connecting with people who have been in your shoes and crossed over to the light of mastering their mornings will give you clear reference points that you *can* succeed at this, just as others who have struggled have. Watching or listening to inspirational and informational content will serve as the informative reminder you need to get started and push through your normal, expected struggles until you've mastered this.

Success Stories

The reason we want to alter our habits is that we have an image of how much more incredibly wonderful our lives can be; how much better WE can be. When we hear stories about successful people who live their lives in accordance with the ways we want to change, it is motivating, inspiring, and gives us a high standard to live up to.

Successful people (whether physically, financially, emotionally, or spiritually successful) often exhibit similar daily patterns, one of which is a well-thought-out and well-practiced morning routine. Getting bits and pieces of information about existing success stories will get you going on those days you don't feel you have it in you; those days where you just don't remember what you're aiming for anymore.

By having a successful icon's morning routine dissected, you can also get ideas for how to improve your own mornings.

We all need motivation, and understanding what it is that creates success for others will not only motivate you, but it will be a constant reminder of what it takes to be great.

Affirmations

Affirmations and visualization are highly effective tools used by some of the most successful people to have ever lived. From athletes to actors to CEOs, affirmations are used to help channel positive energy towards goals and create an inevitable connection between your present self and the end goal you have in mind.

What Affirmations Really Do

1. Unconsciously tap into your creativity muscle to begin generating creative ways of reaching your goals.

2. Unconsciously program your brain to associate yourself with the end goal you have in mind, and prepares you to mentally sort out the steps necessary to get from where you are right now to your end goals.

3. Attract you to your goal by the simple act of envisioning yourself where you ultimately want to be.

4. Motivate you in the sense that it literally causes your brain to believe that you have within you the power, ability and capability to get exactly where you want in life.

So What Does It Mean to Use Affirmations?

Using affirmations is the act of repeating to yourself that you already are the person you want to be.

By envisioning that you can achieve your life goals, you can be exactly the person you ideally envision yourself to be.

It is the repeating of idealistic situations you would like to see yourself in, except you say them in the present tense, as if they were true now.

While repeating these affirmations, you visualize yourself as this ideal person, in the ideal situation you want to see yourself in, which trains your brain to believe it is possible.

Eat That Frog

Knock Out Your Most Important Task of the Day.

Mark Twain once said that if the first thing you do each morning is to eat a LIVE frog you fill yourself with a sense of strength and certainty that you've conquered the most difficult task of your day.

This sense of accomplishment makes you feel incredibly capable in tackling any other difficult tasks you have.

Brian Tracy elaborates on this concept in his amazing book, *Eat That Frog* (productivity nerds - this book is for you).

For the purposes of this journal, your 'frog' is your biggest, most important task of the day - the one you are most likely to procrastinate on if you don't do something about it early on.

 Every day you need to decide what your 'frog' is for the day, and do your best to tackle that frog early on in your schedule. We recommend starting this directly after you complete your morning routine, or first thing when you get into your office.

Seeing how much better your day gets by tackling your 'frog' early is the easiest way to fall in love with the morning. It'll instantly improve your quality of life ten-fold.

Challenge yourself to begin with your largest, most difficult, yet most significant task first. Start it right away, with no breaks, and push through until you complete it before you jump to something else.

Treat this as a test. Think of this as a personal challenge. Beat your temptation to start your day with any easier task.

The world's greatest leaders are each people who jump directly into their life's greatest tasks. They discipline themselves to work laser-focused until those tasks are finished.

Our brains are wired mentally and emotionally in such a way that the act of completing a task floods our brains with happiness.

You chemically reward your brain when you complete any task. You become happier. You feel like a winner. The larger and more difficult/important your task, the larger the impact it will have on your brain.

You will feel more confident. Radiant. More powerful. And ready to conquer the world.

You will quite literally grow a positive, healthy addiction (habit) for your brain to jump into a difficult task and complete it.

You will consistently rush your brain with endorphins. You'll feel mental clarity, confidence, and completeness, daily.

Maintaining the Balance

On each of the tracking pages within the journal, you'll find two separate question types:

 Self-Improvement

 Self-Appreciation

There are ten unique prompts for each, which will rotate as you advance through the journal.

Our goal is to strike the right balance between:

1. Unconditional acceptance for who you are as a person, and
2. The drive to fulfill your potential of living as the best version of yourself.

There's a balance that must occur for this journey to be the most beneficial: While working towards improvement, you'll simultaneously allow yourself to feel fully content and accepting of who you are in this moment. It is a tenuous dance between progressing to who you want to become, yet affording your current-self grace and appreciation.

Keeping that balance is a difficult task that can be extremely rewarding as you'll keep growing without any harsh self-judgement.

The 'How'

Perfectionists, Tread Lightly.
The Importance of Not Getting Caught up with Having "the Perfect/Best" Morning.

Of course, ideally we want to structure our morning in a way that makes the rest of our day flawless. We'd all love to wake up at the perfect time, eat breakfast, exercise, read, write, and meditate all before any of our day's obligations come into play.

But sometimes there's a problem with shooting for perfection from the very start.

Shooting for perfection before you even complete your first morning routine can prevent you from ever taking one step in the direction of your goal.

So often you see people getting caught up in finding the best way to start working out, the best diet to lose weight, the most up-to-date research on the amount of sleep you need to be getting to feel amazing throughout the day…but we'll let you in on a little secret.

There's one simple concept that shatters all the best research, tips, and strategies you can look for (which you'll be getting through this journal).

Here it is… the best way to become a morning person and begin forming a great morning routine is….

You start doing SOMETHING.

You start taking SOME actions towards your goal.

You make SOME effort.

Don't let the desire to reach perfection - the possibility of mastering your morning in a complete and wholesome way, disallow you from making sure you make today's morning better than yesterday.

Don't waste your energy fantasizing and searching.

The best way to determine YOUR ideal morning routine is by trying JUST ONE THING.

Nobody ELSE can tell you how to structure your morning. All they can do is give you information.

It's up to you to try ONE suggestion and move forward from that point. Altering your habits is about investigating what does and doesn't work FOR YOU, not for anyone else.

You'll be getting all the information and motivation you need from us on a daily basis in the form of daily content.

You won't PERSONALLY think every piece of content is useful. You won't think every tip will be effective. You won't think every podcast is insightful. You won't think every affirmation is worthwhile.

But if you make an attempt to use every piece of content, you'll see results. Pinky promise. Disregard the upside you *expect* out of it before trying it — take action first.

Every little action you take propels a snowball effect that greatly impacts other areas of your life.

If you push yourself to do a morning routine for even three days, you're gifting yourself a positive chain of effects that will improve your daily energy, mental clarity, and ability to crush important tasks. This is the true end goal of doing a morning routine, and arguably, of the journal as a whole.

In turn, when you don't prioritize the importance of your mornings, each of these things get sacrificed. Building a consistent healthy morning routine is one of the most powerful tools you have to help you become the best version of yourself as quickly as possible.

Help your body actually experience this so it has a positive reference point instead of just reading words on this page. Break through every obstacle and excuse you may face to absolutely get to bed early tonight and spend 15 minutes tomorrow morning doing any sort of morning routine.

Success is all about taking small, consistent actions over time.

When Should I Wake Up?

5 AM   10 AM

YOU CAN HAVE AN AMAZING MORNING AT ANYTIME

A common misconception is mixing up 'waking up early' with 'doing a morning routine.'

The most important aspect of this is actually doing a daily routine (e.g. reading, exercising, meditating, etc. even if it's only for 5 minutes).

On days that you do not do your outlined rituals in the morning, *still fill out the journal.* As long as they get done, they should be considered completed.

By forcing yourself to take action that will improve your life in the mornings, you set that same tone for the rest of your day.

Whether you start your morning at 5 A.M. or 11 A.M. isn't nearly as important as completing your morning objectives.

Although waking up early can be peaceful, serene, and energizing, that is NOT the main goal of this habit. We will refer to it throughout the journal because it can be very useful, but keep in mind it's not the essential key — daily routines are.

Even if you wake up late, you can still do your routine as part of your day. The main goal here is to just be consistent with what you're doing on a daily basis.

You WILL have days where you're absolutely off, down, and don't feel like 'the best version of yourself.'

These are the **MOST IMPORTANT** days to force yourself to do your daily routine.

This will rewire your brain to understand that it does not matter how incredibly good, utterly bad, or absolutely average your day is going. You WILL get your life habits done regardless.

Think about it:

- You ONLY have something to gain by doing this.
- The world's leaders undoubtedly implement this habit, and they also deal with the ordinary daily struggles we're all faced with.
- You don't lose ANYTHING by trying.

There is no reason for you not to commit to this habit with your heart and soul.

…**Just take the first step.**

Common Challenges
Doing a Morning Routine When You Have a Significant Other

Waking up early and doing a morning routine when you have a significant other can be a challenge. The best solution here, of course, is to have your partner join you in making the change.

If your significant other is not interested in changing their morning routine (which is completely fair and reasonable), there are a couple of action steps you can take to minimize the obstacle of having a partner with a different morning schedule:

- After you write down fill out the 'Why' section in this journal, go ahead and show it to your partner.

- Explain to them how important making this change is to you, and that although you understand if they don't want to join you, you are fully committed to becoming an early riser with a well-intentioned morning routine.

- Specifically tell them that you would really appreciate if they helped to keep you motivated throughout the process and reminded you how important this goal is to you when you're feeling discouraged.

Essentially, let your partner know how much you would appreciate them being a positive force in making this change! The more specific you are about things that they can do to help you, or NOT do that might hurt your chances of waking up early or doing your routine, the easier it will be for them to be that positive force you need.

Doing a Morning Routine When You Work at Night

First of all - if you're the type of warrior who bought this journal when you work into the night, you're awesome.

Second, we want to emphasize that waking up early is a relative concept.

The point of this journal and incorporating the habit of waking up early and doing a morning routine is to begin your day intentionally, and before you 'have to' start the day.

If you start your ordinary day at 7 a.m., then waking up 'early' means starting the day before 7 o'clock with enough time to do a morning routine that will set you up for the perfect day. The same applies if you start your day at 4 or 5 p.m.

Staying focused on being intentional about what you do when you get up (before the obligations of the day begin) is the goal.

Doing a Morning Routine When You Have Kids

Many, many of the wonderful people who have had success with this journal have children. Being a parent is possibly the most perfect reason for establishing a morning routine. The benefits are numerous, but the biggest positive comes in the form of guaranteed alone-time. This snowballs wonderfully into feeling in control of your day.

If you have children and you're making this effort of waking up early and doing a morning routine, there are a couple of things to keep in mind.

If you want to wake up early, it's very important to get to bed at a reasonable hour, especially if you have kids. Having a no-negotiation lights out time for yourself (if possible) is vital.

Depending on how old your children are and what your morning routine consists of, you can incorporate them into parts of your morning routine in different ways.

Try to be creative with it! If your children are old enough, doing activities together to start the day will help them naturally understand how important it is to start the day intentionally and calmly before the madness of the day begins. Plus, it's incredible quality time you spend together.

We've had many stories from customers who talk about how valuable it is to have some time alone in the morning without the kids.

We've also received stories from mothers who do their morning routine with their kids (things like stretching, meditating, reading), a practice they've found has positively impacted working on their habits together with their children.

If you put some thought into it, you WILL make it work. Use your 'Why' to guide your morning decision making.

Balancing Your Morning Routine with Your Social Life

It is, of course, important to have a relatively consistent sleep/wake-up schedule so your body knows what to expect on a daily basis, but having quality social time with friends and family is also a vital part of living a happy, well-balanced life.

All it takes to deal with this obstacle is re-framing the way you think about it and preparing beforehand.

The next time a social event comes up, all you need to do is change the time you're going to wake up to match the new time you're going to bed that night, and adjust your morning routine for the next day to fit the amount of time you allow yourself in the morning.

Basically, you shift everything back based on the time you're going to wake up, and if needed, make adjustments to your morning routine to fit the time you have.

To make this a HABIT, you have to stay **intentional** about your mornings regardless of the circumstances. But you also have to be malleable in terms of how you approach it.

If you have to skip the morning routine altogether because you won't be able to get enough rest otherwise, then accept that and move forward. Accept it wholeheartedly and without guilt.

The danger is when one or two nights becomes a week or longer. Momentum must then be created again, which we all know is very difficult. So, remain intentional, and **if you're going to take the day off**, do it with the understanding that **you'll pick it right back up the next day!**

Holding Yourself Accountable

Using the Journal

Each morning after getting out of bed, **put your journal on your pillow.** This will create a very easy trigger to remind you to use your journal and plan your next morning. If you choose not to, it will need to be a much more conscious decision of physically picking the journal up and setting it aside to instead of merely ignoring it on your nightstand.

The journal itself is also designed to create an accountability loop. At night, you map out and write out your morning routine. And in the mornings, you plan out the rest of your day and night. This creates an engaging cycle of accountability for yourself.

Staying Consistent

One of the best ways to continue doing this habit is to build it alongside a friend who is also passionate about becoming the best version of themself. Having someone to talk to and brainstorm about your specific pain points makes a huge difference. A friend's support (and sometimes competitive kick) can serve as a nice backup too.

Getting to Bed on Time

A huge part of mastering your mornings falls on getting to bed on time the night before. Let's be real. THIS IS REALLY HARD. So how do we do this?

By setting clear boundaries - you *MUST* clarify your 'lights out' time. This is especially useful to jump-start this habit.

First, determine your wake-up time *(let's say 5 A.M.)*. Next, subtract how many hours you want to sleep *(let's assume 7 hours. So lights out time is 10 P.M.)*. **Boom** - rocket science, complete.

The Power of Accountability

Think about yourself over the last month — how many of those days could you say you lived as the absolute best version of yourself?

For many of us, the answer to that question is not as great as it could be. We all have ways of improving this over time, though having a source of external accountability can make ALL the difference in staying consistent with our goals.

It's so much easier to give in to our emotional needs and our shifting desires than it is to be disciplined, at all times.

However, this completely changes if we have somebody else checking in on us and specifically asking about the decisions we're making. Not in a guilt-inducing way whatsoever, but much more as a mirror reflecting the best version of ourselves and what we're capable of… as a real-world reminder that letting yourself down is something that you will have to think about and face later.

This is why we created our own accountability service, *Accountability Nest*, where a military veteran will hold you accountable to your goals every day.

Our coaches are people who have not only built discipline in their own life to a large degree, but who, at the same time, are incredibly empathetic about other people and working with their individualized needs.

They'll reverse-engineer whether you're the type of person who thrives better under tough-love, under a more supportive environment, or a mix of the two.

They're very passionate to build up the discipline in yourself so you won't need to work with them for the long-run.

If this is something that interests you, you can learn more here: **habitnest.com/accountability**

Addressing Hard Days Ahead

Important: **You do not need to finish this journal in 66 consecutive calendar days in order for it to be effective!**

In fact, practically every single person who has prepared a morning routine has failed to follow it at some point.

Instead of trying to gloss over this, we're choosing to take a more practical approach by preparing specifically for those days of failure that will most likely blindside you when you least expect it (e.g. when your motivation is high or something sneaks up on you).

There are two keys to using these struggle days in a way that will benefit you:

First, empathize with yourself in that situation. Don't just think about it, actually *feel* what you'd be experiencing (e.g. if you were very motivated and one day you slipped up). Put yourself in that headspace.

Second, write out what the most disciplined version of yourself would do in that state, post-failure. Some examples of what your most disciplined self might do:

- Remove all guilt as you realize it's useless. Instead, you immediately search for WHY this happened.

- You get genuinely excited to keep going because you realize that you love challenges - each one you surpass makes you a stronger person.

- Moving forward, you're mentally equipped with all you need to not let this specific mistake happen again.

- You realize this is a completely normal part of the self-improvement process - you gather all your energy, recoup mentally, and attack your day regardless.

Now, for the first time you truly struggle - what would you tell yourself and what would your actions be?

_____

_____

_____

_____

_____

_____

_____

When you face your first struggle point, you don't need to do this exactly as you've written. However, having this as a reference point will prove quite useful in that moment.

Morning Routine Suggestions
Let's Get Focused

There isn't a right answer to exactly how you should set up your morning. The key is to have a very real understanding of what you want to get out of it.

Your morning routine should bring about a specific outcome in your life. For example, it could be to create energy and momentum for your day or to knock out 1-2 of your most important tasks early on.

To get full clarity on this, write out what you want out of your mornings. What should they set your day up for?

_____

_____

_____

_____

_____

_____

_____

Examples of What You Can Do with Your Mornings

For every activity that you put in your mornings, ask if it'll bring about the outcome you identified above or not.

It's also completely okay to experiment here — you can test different activities in your mornings which will likely change as time goes on. Here are some popular choices:

- Exercise
- Meditate
- Read
- Write or journal
- Work on a side project
- Get work done that you otherwise have to do later
- Spend time with loved ones
- Eat a good breakfast
- Do some household chores
- Go for a walk and listen to a podcast

These are all typical examples of the ways 'morning people' start their days. You can create a routine by choosing your favorite actions from the above or creating your own.

You can do whatever you want with your morning as long as it's furthering your goals, your desires, and your life in a way that will impact your future positively.

Most 'morning people' (a.k.a. anybody who has simply built this habit) create their routine around this concept.

Sample Journal Page

Night 0

(Begin Nighttime Routine.)

TONIGHT I'LL SLEEP AT: <u>11:00pm</u> & TOMORROW I'LL WAKE UP AT: <u>6:30am</u>

 MEMORABLE MOMENT(S) I EXPERIENCED TODAY:

Watching the sunrise on my morning run :)

Finally made time to clean out the house!

☀ **MY MORNING RITUAL TOMORROW WILL BE:**   *Completed?*

1. 5 minutes of meditation   ☑
2. Read 2 pages of "Think and Grow Rich"   ☑
3. Affirmations   ☐
4. Walk 2 blocks outside   ☐
5. Plan out and strategize the rest of my day   ☐

Day 1

(Begin Morning Routine.)

LAST NIGHT I SLEPT AT: <u>11:30pm</u> & WOKE UP TODAY AT: <u>6:30am</u>

 MY MOST IMPORTANT TASK FOR TODAY IS:

Begin my new marketing project at work!

🎯 **ONE SMALL WAY I CAN IMPROVE MYSELF IS:**

Less Facebook / Instagram in the mornings

🧘 **TOP TWO DISTRACTIONS TO MINIMIZE TONIGHT (BEFORE BED):**

1. Watching YouTube in bed (limit: 15mins)
2. Watching the news (limit: 15mins)

A Simple Idea

We hope that after reading the introductory pages, you're motivated and ready to tackle tomorrow morning with every ounce of energy you have.

We'll leave you to it with one simple idea.

Tomorrow, you will be exactly who you are **today**.

The rest of your life is a future projection of who you are today.

If you **change** today, tomorrow will be **different**.

If you **don't change** today, the rest of your life is **pre-determined**.

Commit.

No matter what happens tomorrow...

*whether I am exhausted
or have the **worst** day of my life...*

*...whether I win the lottery
or have the **best** day of my life...*

*I **will** do my morning
routine for the next week.*

*My word is like **gold**.*

*I will do whatever it takes
to make this happen.*

I **will** do my morning routine this week (circle one):

On Weekdays Only   **Every Damn Day**

_____   _____

Signature   Date

PHASE 1:

DAYS 1-7

Phase 1	Phase 2	Phase 3
Days 01-07	Days 08-21	Days 22-66+
Hell Week.	Staying Consistent.	Rewiring Your Brain.

Phase 1: Hell Week

When beginning a new habit, what's really important is getting to the point where you start to see the benefits you expect. Starting won't be easy.. You need to believe in yourself and take at least one concrete step in the direction of your goal every single day during this phase because it's really easy to lose hope right off the bat.

Make use of every tip, every affirmation, and all the motivation you're getting to make it as easy as possible to take just one action towards your goal every day. Remember, we want to get to the point where we see benefits, and from that point on, self-motivation to re-acquire those benefits comes into play and smooths out the process.

Let's do this.

WAIT! Have you gone through the intro pages of this journal yet? If not, skim through them now! They're quick to go through and imperative to really conquering this habit.

Day 1: **Pro-Tip**

Your morning ritual starts the night before.

Your nighttime ritual before each morning is very powerful. If your nighttimes are off, your mornings will inevitably suffer.

All the extra decision-making you usually do in the morning can be done the night before. You don't want to become fatigued by small decisions before the day even starts.

One of the most useful nighttime rituals is preparing for your morning the night before. By removing any extra decisions from your morning, you will be able to wake up with full mental clarity and fly. Experiment with implementing these steps listed below.

Each night, complete the following before going to bed:
1. Picking out your clothes
2. Choosing what you want to eat for breakfast
3. Getting your bag(s) together
4. The first task or ritual you will knock out when your day begins - this should be a task that you absolutely have to get done without question

"Lose an hour in the morning, and you will be all day hunting for it."
- Richard Whately

48

DATE

TONIGHT I'LL SLEEP AT: _____ & TOMORROW I'LL WAKE UP AT: _____

Night 0

(Begin
Nighttime
Routine.)

**WHAT IS ONE UNIQUE THING ABOUT ME
THAT MAKES ME INCREDIBLY SPECIAL?**

_____

MY MORNING RITUAL TOMORROW WILL BE:

Completed?

1. _____ ☐
2. _____ ☐
3. _____ ☐
4. _____ ☐
5. _____ ☐

(Write the actual times).

LAST NIGHT I SLEPT AT: _____ & WOKE UP TODAY AT: _____

(Check these
off in the
morning!)

Day 1

(Begin
Morning
Routine.)

MY MOST IMPORTANT TASK FOR TODAY IS:

_____

WHAT IS ONE WAY I AM NOT FULLY LIVING UP TO MY POTENTIAL?

_____

TOP TWO DISTRACTIONS TO MINIMIZE TONIGHT (BEFORE BED):

1. _____
2. _____

Day 2: **Daily Challenge**

Challenge: Use off days to rewire your brain by doing your habit when you LEAST 'feel' like it.

The next time you wake up feeling tired or stressed is when it's MOST important to wake up and start the day out the way you planned it. This tells your brain: "This is happening. Nothing can get in my way. I'm unstoppable."

Newsflash: Your morning routine doesn't have to be "the best that it can be." Not even close.

You're going to have days where you feel OFF. The importance is actually doing it anyway. **No more excuses, just start your routine (even if it's done <u>horribly</u>).** _The goal: train your body to adopt the habit, even on off days._ <u>**This is one of the biggest keys to succeeding.**</u>

You'll _only **FEEL**_ like doing your morning routine when you're in a positive mindset. **That's nonsense.**

Pick one option - you either get it done or you don't. _One or zero._ Use every ounce of energy you have to get it done. **Make today a <u>one</u>.** _Zero_ isn't an option.

(Note: Anything not match up to your expectations for the journal? Email us at support@habitnest.com so we can make it right.)

_____
DATE

Night 1

TONIGHT I'LL SLEEP AT: _____ & TOMORROW I'LL WAKE UP AT: _____

WHAT IS A CHALLENGE - BIG OR SMALL - I'VE SUCCESSFULLY MOVED PAST TODAY?

_____

MY MORNING RITUAL TOMORROW WILL BE:

Completed?

(Make these SMALL! e.g. read 2 pages, not 10 pages.)

1. _____ ☐
2. _____ ☐
3. _____ ☐
4. _____ ☐
5. _____ ☐

Day 2

LAST NIGHT I SLEPT AT: _____ & WOKE UP TODAY AT: _____

MY MOST IMPORTANT TASK FOR TODAY IS:

_____

(Reminder: This journal doesn't have to be completed in 66 calendar days! If you miss a day or more, resume when ready.)

WHAT IS AN AREA OF WEAKNESS I HAVE IN MY LIFE THAT I WANT TO IMPROVE ON?

_____

(Try setting a generous yet specific time limit for these.)

TOP TWO DISTRACTIONS TO MINIMIZE TONIGHT (BEFORE BED):

1. _____
2. _____

Day 3: **Pro-Tip**

Condition yourself week-by-week to shift your wake-up time.

Make the process of reaching your ideal wake-up time with a morning routine a true transition. If you all of a sudden decide to start waking up 5 hours earlier than you normally do, it isn't too realistic to expect that your body won't make that change within a couple days.

Start off by shifting your waking time by 15 or 30 minutes a day until you reach your goal. We would recommend even improving your wake-up time by 15-30 minutes every **week.**

Small victories are one of the keys to success. This applies to anything in life, but can be used specifically for easing into altering your wake-up time.

It may feel less rewarding initially, but if you try to make a dramatic change all at once, chances are you'll hit a wall, ruin your workday on multiple occasions, and consequently become discouraged. Make your goals attainable without shocking your body and really try to condition yourself in a natural and holistic way.

"Opportunities are like sunrises. If you wait too long, you miss them."
- William Arthur Ward

DATE _____

Night 2

TONIGHT I'LL SLEEP AT: _____ & TOMORROW I'LL WAKE UP AT: _____

WHAT IS A SKILL I'VE BUILT IN MY LIFE THAT I USED TO MY BENEFIT TODAY?

(Self-Appreciation Prompt)

_____

MY MORNING RITUAL TOMORROW WILL BE:

Completed?

(By making these small, you're making it insanely easy to succeed.)

1. _____ ☐
2. _____ ☐
3. _____ ☐
4. _____ ☐
5. _____ ☐

Day 3

LAST NIGHT I SLEPT AT: _____ & WOKE UP TODAY AT: _____

MY MOST IMPORTANT TASK FOR TODAY IS:

(This can be completed any time, not just the mornings.)

_____

WHO IS ONE PERSON WHO I CAN GIVE EXTRA CARE AND ATTENTION TO TODAY?

(Self-Improvement Prompt)

_____

TOP TWO DISTRACTIONS TO MINIMIZE TONIGHT (BEFORE BED):

1. _____
2. _____

Day 4: **Daily Challenge**

Challenge: Write down what factors have recently impeded you from successfully performing your morning routine.

Envision the most recent time you completely 'failed' at your morning routine or had some other negative experience with it.

Now breathe… Everybody (and we mean **_everybody_**) struggles with consistency. The truth is that imperfect days teach us the most about how to succeed.

Treat days you mess up as experiments. By consciously writing down what factors caused us to struggle, we can better prepare against them.

On days you aren't 'perfect', try to answer these questions:

1. What was my thought process during the first decision I made that led me astray from having an even better day? What can I learn from this to apply moving forward?
2. In addition to the above, what are some additional 'rules' you can set to prevent what caused this specific slip-up in the future?
3. What justification did you tell yourself to make it okay to slip up?

These mental insights can really act as secret weapons on days we struggle. We will all miss doing our habits. Let's make those days just as valuable as perfect days by treating them as learning experiences.

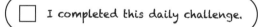
☐ I completed this daily challenge.

(Life hack: If you use this journal's elastic band to hold it closed, the band doubles up as a pen holder. Slide your pen clip through it, allowing your pen to rest on top of the book!)

DATE _____

TONIGHT I'LL SLEEP AT: _____ & TOMORROW I'LL WAKE UP AT: _____

Night 3

WHAT IS ONE THING I DID TODAY THAT WILL HAVE A CHAIN-EFFECT OF SPREADING POSITIVITY?

_____

MY MORNING RITUAL TOMORROW WILL BE:

Completed?

(Use your nights to keep yourself accountable in the mornings.)

1. _____ ☐
2. _____ ☐
3. _____ ☐
4. _____ ☐
5. _____ ☐

Day 4

LAST NIGHT I SLEPT AT: _____ & WOKE UP TODAY AT: _____

MY MOST IMPORTANT TASK FOR TODAY IS:

_____

IF I WERE LIVING AS THE ABSOLUTE BEST VERSION OF MYSELF, WHAT CAN I CHANGE ABOUT MY ACTIONS TODAY?

(GUILT is a discipline destroyer. Don't be perfect, be practical.)

_____

(And your mornings to hold yourself accountable at night!)

TOP TWO DISTRACTIONS TO MINIMIZE TONIGHT (BEFORE BED):

1. _____
2. _____

Day 5: **Pro-Tip**

Find a morning accountability partner.

Having someone holding you accountable to your goals is a powerful force that can serve as one of the strongest assets in your journey. It lets you have an additional pair of eyes on your own behavior, instills you with an even stronger sense of responsibility, and can often help the other person stay committed to their own goals as well.

1. Find someone as ambitious as you are that can serve as an accountability partner.
   a. Note: find someone who shares your goal - if you are a night owl who simply wants to have a more proactive routine rather than waking up earlier, finding someone who shares that vision will serve as a much better partner for you.
2. Select a goal wake-up time.
3. Pick a method of evidence.
   a. Send them a text/selfie of waking up.
   b. Call them when you're up.

PS We created an intimate community and accountability group online to discuss habits here: facebook.com/groups/habitnest/

Superhero Option: *Determine what time you and your partner want to wake up. Only one of you sets an alarm so you know the other is counting on you to wake them up!*

"I'm always craving that dreamy creative energy I can only get while the rest of the world is asleep." - Lindsay Champion

Night 4

TONIGHT I'LL SLEEP AT: _____ & TOMORROW I'LL WAKE UP AT: _____

IF A CLOSE FRIEND SAW HOW I HANDLED MY DAY TODAY, WHAT WOULD THEY TELL ME?

_____

(These should be so easy to do, it should feel almost like a joke to hit your minimums.)

MY MORNING RITUAL TOMORROW WILL BE:

Completed?

1. _____ ☐
2. _____ ☐
3. _____ ☐
4. _____ ☐
5. _____ ☐

Day 5

LAST NIGHT I SLEPT AT: _____ & WOKE UP TODAY AT: _____

MY MOST IMPORTANT TASK FOR TODAY IS:

(Starting your day for 5min with this = huge win.)

_____

WHAT CAUSES ME STRESS AND HOW COULD I BETTER RESPOND TO IT?

_____

(Note: These distractions are okay to have - but own them by being mindful of them.)

TOP TWO DISTRACTIONS TO MINIMIZE TONIGHT (BEFORE BED):

1. _____
2. _____

Day 6: **Pro-Tip**

Some strategies for chronic snoozers.

Snoozing can be an incredibly difficult habit to break or overcome. Here are some tips that you can try (or combine for maximum effectiveness):

1. Make it a rule not to turn off your alarm until you've **stepped out of bed** and are standing up.

2. Learn exactly the right amount of sleep you need (hours-wise) to have a fantastic day. You need to experiment with what that number is for you. Once you have it though, you should set your go to bed and wake-up times based on that.

   Now when your alarm goes off, you can have **_trust and respect_** for it, based on the times you set. Even if you're tired in that moment, you'll know deep down that (if set correctly) you got the right amount of sleep and there's no value for you to sleep in.

3. Realize that it's **perfectly okay to be tired when you get** up in the morning. Instead, you can allow your body to wake up as you begin your day and morning routine. Remember, start moving!

"If you really think about it, hitting the snooze button in the morning doesn't even make sense. It's like saying, 'I hate getting up in the morning—so I do it over... and over... and over again." - Demetri Martin

DATE _____

Night 5

TONIGHT I'LL SLEEP AT: _____ & TOMORROW I'LL WAKE UP AT: _____

WHAT AM I GREAT AT THAT I DON'T GIVE MYSELF ENOUGH CREDIT FOR?

_____

MY MORNING RITUAL TOMORROW WILL BE:

Completed?

(Being consistent is about 1000x more important than how WELL you do these.)

1. _____ ☐
2. _____ ☐
3. _____ ☐
4. _____ ☐
5. _____ ☐

Day 6

LAST NIGHT I SLEPT AT: _____ & WOKE UP TODAY AT: _____

MY MOST IMPORTANT TASK FOR TODAY IS:

_____

IF I WERE TO MAKE NO EXCUSES FOR MY LIFE, WHAT WOULD I DO DIFFERENTLY?

_____

TOP TWO DISTRACTIONS TO MINIMIZE TONIGHT (BEFORE BED):

(Don't feel guilty if you don't hit these predictions. Instead, investigate WHY you didn't.)

1. _____
2. _____

59

Day 7: **Favorite Resources**

Alarmy Alarm Clock App.
Cost: Free. Available on both iOS and Android.
Note: we have no affiliation with *Alarmy*. We just love their app.

Alarmy is the self-proclaimed 'most annoying alarm app in the world' and it is the most downloaded alarm clock application on the planet.

It has different options for getting you out of bed, like:

1. Registering a photo of an area or room in your house. Then once the alarm is set, the only way to make it stop ringing is to get out of bed and go take a photo of the registered area.

2. Using the Shake Model, you shake your phone until you reach your preset goal to dismiss the alarm.

3. Solving math problems to stop your alarm with the option of customizing the level of difficulty and number of questions to solve in the morning.

It's pretty interesting and if you're the type of person who is always going to have difficulty just getting out of the bed, the app could work really well for you!

THE ALARMY APP

"It is well to be up before daybreak, for such habits contribute to health, wealth, and wisdom." - Aristotle

DATE _____

Night 6

TONIGHT I'LL SLEEP AT: _____ & TOMORROW I'LL WAKE UP AT: _____

🤝 HOW HAVE I POSITIVELY IMPACTED SOMEONE'S LIFE TODAY?

_____

☀️ MY MORNING RITUAL TOMORROW WILL BE:

Completed?

1. _____ ☐
2. _____ ☐
3. _____ ☐
4. _____ ☐
5. _____ ☐

Day 7

LAST NIGHT I SLEPT AT: _____ & WOKE UP TODAY AT: _____

🐎 MY MOST IMPORTANT TASK FOR TODAY IS:

_____

◉ WHERE IS ONE PLACE I AM SPENDING TIME THAT DOES NOT BRING ME REAL HAPPINESS?

_____

🧘 TOP TWO DISTRACTIONS TO MINIMIZE TONIGHT (BEFORE BED):

1. _____
2. _____

PHASE 1:

CONQUERED.

Phase 1 Recap: Days 1-7

1. What morning rituals do you want to continue doing?

_____

_____

2. What rituals were not useful for you that you'll cut?

_____

_____

3. What are some new rituals you want to experiment with?

_____

_____

4. If you continued this habit for another 2 weeks, what kind of person would you become?

_____

_____

_____

5. If you dropped this habit now, would it benefit your life in any way?

_____

_____

_____

PHASE 2:

DAYS 8-21

 ~~Phase 1~~ **Phase 2** Phase 3

~~Days 01-07~~ **Days 08-21** Days 22-66+
~~Hell Week.~~ **Staying Consistent.** Rewiring Your Brain.

Phase 2: Digging Deep - Staying Consistent

Congratulations, you've gotten through Phase 1 (Hell Week)!

If you don't feel like you've made as much progress as you'd like, don't worry. One day and one victory at a time is the key.

Phase 2 is important because this is the point where we either feel like we've got it down, OR we feel hopeless that we'll never reach our goals. Either way, ignore what your mind says.

If you feel like you've reached your goal, don't trust the feeling because now you need to STAY consistent. Don't let your guard down. And if you feel hopeless, you won't feel hopeless forever as long as you continue to believe in yourself and make a real effort daily.

Note: this phase features a **new section** in place of distractions - **benefits**! These can help you stay consistent by seeing what you're GAINING from doing your routine daily.

One huge thing to watch out for: On days people miss routines, many people end up circling 0 benefits that day. This leads them to feeling like they scored a '0/6' that day and are naturally bad at this (which they're not, everybody misses days), and thus use it as a trigger to fall off the wagon.
Be mindful of this on days you struggle and **stick with it!**

Commit.

I KNOW this next phase
is going to be extremely hard.

I understand I may not
be perfect about it every day.

*But I **will** put my heart, each day, into*
conquering this life-changing goal.

If I miss a day,
I will pick back up.

Off days and missed days
will NEVER stop me.

In the long-run,
I will win.

_____

*I **will** complete Phase 2 of this journal.*

_____   _____

Signature   Date

Phase 1 Medal
Earned!

Day 8: **Daily Challenge**

_Challenge: **Pay attention to the mini decisions you make.
Ask yourself, "If I made this choice EVERY DAY, would I be a lot
closer to my goals, or a lot further?"**_

Newsflash: **Your choices are 100 times more important than you
think.** Every choice you make today is building up a habit for the rest
of your life. Our brains learn from what we do repeatedly - the
decision to oversleep is in reality 100x more powerful over time.

Taking one tiny action in a positive direction has the same effect.
From little things, like waking up 5 minutes earlier — to big things
like doing an important task first thing in the morning or pushing
through that last rep of your workout when you have nothing left in
the tank. This snowballs over time into the person you are becoming.

You can justify not doing your habit, but your mind and body grow
accustomed to it. Creating excuses is a mental habit that can
absolutely be rewired. Your brain only knows **what you do**. When
you start the day with intention, your brain rewires itself. _**All mini-
decisions build up to your habits.** **You _are_ your mini-decisions.**_

> ☐ I completed this daily challenge.

DON'T STOP.
THIS IS YOUR
LAST REP!

_"Don't let the old you make your decisions. Today is the only day change
exists. Change today and your entire life will be altered. Don't change
today, and tomorrow will be exactly like today, forever." - Ari Banayan_

Night 7

TONIGHT I'LL SLEEP AT: _____ & TOMORROW I'LL WAKE UP AT: _____

WHAT IS SOMETHING I SPENT TIME ON TODAY THAT COULD POSITIVELY IMPACT MY FUTURE?

(Phase 2 is a great time to revisit your 'Why' on page 5.)

_____

BENEFITS I FELT TODAY (CIRCLE):

Feel Happier · More Organized · Fuller Day · Increased Productivity · More Energized · Reduced Stress

MY MORNING RITUAL TOMORROW WILL BE:

Completed?

(Try combining a few simpler steps into one line, e.g. brush teeth + shower + bathroom.)

1. _____ ☐
2. _____ ☐
3. _____ ☐
4. _____ ☐
5. _____ ☐

Day 8

LAST NIGHT I SLEPT AT: _____ & WOKE UP TODAY AT: _____

MY MOST IMPORTANT TASK FOR TODAY IS:

_____

WHO IS ONE CONTENT CREATOR OR AUTHOR I CAN REVISIT OR LEARN MORE FROM TO IMPROVE MY LIFE?

_____

Day 9: **Super Read**

<u>Title:</u> *The Miracle Morning*
<u>Author</u>: Hal Elrod

The Miracle Morning is an incredible book about creating the best morning routine on the planet. Hal's life story is pretty amazing, having survived a car crash that left him dead for six minutes.

This book will help you jumpstart your mornings by implementing a morning routine called the Life S.A.V.E.R.S. Hal breaks down into specific actionable steps how to implement Silence (meditation), Affirmations, Visualization, Exercise, Reading, and Scribing (writing/journaling).

We could not recommend this book more highly as it has transformed how we master our mornings daily.

Where to get it: Search "Miracle Morning" on Amazon.

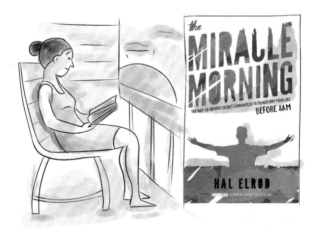

"The moment you accept responsibility for EVERYTHING in your life is the moment you can change ANYTHING in your life." - Hal Elrod

DATE _____

Night 8

TONIGHT I'LL SLEEP AT: _____ & TOMORROW I'LL WAKE UP AT: _____

WHAT IS ONE EMOTIONAL RESPONSE I HAD TODAY THAT I AM PROUD OF?

_____

(If your weekdays/ weekends fluctuate, feel free to create different routines & wake-up times for each.)

⊘ **BENEFITS I FELT TODAY (CIRCLE):**

😊 Feel Happier

More Organized

Fuller Day

Increased Productivity

More Energized

Reduced Stress

(Setting TINY, EASILY ACHIEVABLE daily goals is one of the greatest discipline hacks out there.)

MY MORNING RITUAL TOMORROW WILL BE: *Completed?*

1. _____ ☐
2. _____ ☐
3. _____ ☐
4. _____ ☐
5. _____ ☐

Day 9

LAST NIGHT I SLEPT AT: _____ & WOKE UP TODAY AT: _____

MY MOST IMPORTANT TASK FOR TODAY IS:

_____

WHAT IS ONE TIME I WANT TO BE MORE PRESENT AND LESS DISTRACTED DURING MY DAY?

_____

71

Day 10: **Pro-Tip**

Re-boot your sleep schedule.

If you are sleeping very late (and it's something you're unhappy about), chances are your brain is wired to get consistent dopamine rushes and immediate gratification that keep you awake.

That's okay, this is very common and easy to fix. <u>Take these steps</u>:

1. Set an alarm for 5 hours after your go-to-bed time. When your alarm goes off tomorrow, JUMP out of bed. Be OKAY with the tiredness — this will last a few hours and will fade.
2. Later that day, you will be tired once again. Use this to your advantage to fall asleep early tomorrow night. Do not nap.
3. Set a clear 'lights out' time. When this time comes, shut off all electronics (airplane mode), lights, & distractions.
4. Two options: either read a book or listen to a podcast (download it so it's available offline, in airplane mode) until you fall asleep.

This is the quick, _one-time hack_ to reboot your sleeping schedule to help you sleep earlier. If you've got your sleeping routine down, waking up on time + doing a morning routine will follow.

"If you wake up and you're not looking forward to the day ahead, you need to re-evaluate your life." - Ari Banayan

Night 9

DATE _____

TONIGHT I'LL SLEEP AT: _____ & TOMORROW I'LL WAKE UP AT: _____

HOW HAS MY OUTLOOK ON LIFE IMPROVED MY DAY?

_____

(For added accountability, put your journal on your pillow after each morning routine.)

BENEFITS I FELT TODAY (CIRCLE):

Feel Happier   More Organized   Fuller Day   Increased Productivity   More Energized   Reduced Stress

MY MORNING RITUAL TOMORROW WILL BE: Completed?

(You don't always have to fill in 5 things here, it's up to you.)

1. _____ ☐
2. _____ ☐
3. _____ ☐
4. _____ ☐
5. _____ ☐

Day 10

LAST NIGHT I SLEPT AT: _____ & WOKE UP TODAY AT: _____

MY MOST IMPORTANT TASK FOR TODAY IS:

_____

WHEN WAS THE LAST TIME I DID NOT STICK TO MY WORD? HOW CAN I AVOID DOING SO AGAIN?

_____

Day 11: **Affirmations**

1. Find a quiet area where you can do this in private so you can be at ease. If you can't find a private space, say these in your head while pretending you're screaming them from a mountaintop.

2. Think of a time when you felt absolutely powerful - **when you felt on top of the world**. Tap into every emotion you had at that moment and get yourself into that state right now. How were you feeling then - Powerful? Unstoppable? Strong? Incredible!? Get into it now!!!!

3. Now feel your intensity grow tenfold! Say this with deep passion:

I have limitless drive and energy because I wake up at ____ A.M. Waking up proactively gives me the time to optimize my body and mind before the day starts. Starting the day while the rest of the world is still asleep fills me with incredible confidence, energy and enthusiasm! I am truly unstoppable!!

Repeat this **one more time.**

"When you arise in the morning, think of what a precious privilege it is to be alive - to breathe, to think, to enjoy, to love - then make that day count!" - Steve Maraboli

(Try experimenting with how many hours of sleep you actually need. Test a different number for 3 days straight starting today. Don't go below 7 hrs.)

DATE _____

Night 10

TONIGHT I'LL SLEEP AT: _____ & TOMORROW I'LL WAKE UP AT: _____

HOW HAVE I SET MY FUTURE SELF UP FOR SUCCESS TODAY?

_____

(Remember: it's normal to have off-days and miss these.)

BENEFITS I FELT TODAY (CIRCLE):

Feel Happier | More Organized | Fuller Day | Increased Productivity | More Energized | Reduced Stress

MY MORNING RITUAL TOMORROW WILL BE: *Completed?*

(No guilt allowed for missing these! Only learning.)

1. _____ ☐
2. _____ ☐
3. _____ ☐
4. _____ ☐
5. _____ ☐

Day 11

LAST NIGHT I SLEPT AT: _____ & WOKE UP TODAY AT: _____

MY MOST IMPORTANT TASK FOR TODAY IS:

_____

WHAT IS ONE AREA I CAN APPROACH WITH MORE ENTHUSIASM AND ENERGY TODAY?

_____

Day 12: **Success Story** ♟

Arianna Huffington: Founder of Huffington Post & Thrive Global

Arianna is a superwoman. Her story begins with her being sleep deprived and overworking to exhaustion - to the point that she *passed out on the table and broke her cheekbone.* She now makes it a priority to allow herself ample rest and recovery time, despite how hard she works.

In the morning, she avoids using her phone and instead jumps into exercise and meditation. She skips breakfast in place of coffee, too.

One big takeaway from Arianna is how strongly she uses her nighttime routine to her advantage. By turning off all electronics and moving them out of the room, she allows herself to fully focus on sleep at night.

Oftentimes, one of the most rewarding obstacles to conquer is getting to bed on time and minimizing unnecessary distractions at night. Are there any changes you can make to your nighttime routine that would make a big impact on your mornings?

"When I'm tempted to skip my morning routine or another form of self-care, I remind myself that I can better serve the people I love and the projects I care about when I start with me." – Courtney Carver

Night 11

TONIGHT I'LL SLEEP AT: _____ & TOMORROW I'LL WAKE UP AT: _____

HOW HAVE I SHOWN SELF-LOVE AND CARE TO MYSELF TODAY?

_____

BENEFITS I FELT TODAY (CIRCLE):

Feel Happier   More Organized   Fuller Day   Increased Productivity   More Energized   Reduced Stress

MY MORNING RITUAL TOMORROW WILL BE: Completed?

(If it's helpful, you can write in the times you expect to do each of these as well.)

1. _____ ☐
2. _____ ☐
3. _____ ☐
4. _____ ☐
5. _____ ☐

Day 12

LAST NIGHT I SLEPT AT: _____ & WOKE UP TODAY AT: _____

MY MOST IMPORTANT TASK FOR TODAY IS:

_____

WHO IS SOMEONE THAT WILL HAVE A POSITIVE EFFECT IN MY LIFE THAT I SHOULD SPEND MORE TIME WITH?

_____

(Follow the chain of effects that cause your off-days. Where did it all start from?)

Day 13: **Double Pro-Tip** 💡💡

Drink a glass of ice cold water & play your favorite upbeat music right when you get up.

When you wake up after a night of sleep, your body is naturally dehydrated. Drinking water as soon as you wake-up provides your cells with much needed nourishment & energy. One glass of water will wake you up, instantly fire up your metabolism, flush out unnecessary toxins, fuel your brain and suppress your appetite.

1. Have a glass sitting next to your fridge for your morning water .

Also, when you're groggy or tired, you need a shock to your system to really wake up. Loud music provides that shock to get your mind and body rolling.

2. Play your favorite upbeat, fast tempo music right when you wake up! Keep headphones by your bed so you can play them as loudly as you feel comfortable with (and that won't deafen you).

The best way to do this is to create a playlist with at least 10 different songs so you don't get desensitized to it at all.

Superhero Option: Another shock to your system that works well is doing 10-20 seconds of an exercise as soon as you get out of bed. You can try doing 10 jumping jacks or pushups and you'll instantly be more awake.

"The sun has not caught me in bed in fifty years." - Thomas Jefferson

(Important reminder: The days you DON'T FEEL like doing the journal are the MOST IMPORTANT days to do them! It shows your brain that you're unstoppable.)

DATE _____

Night 12

TONIGHT I'LL SLEEP AT: _____ & TOMORROW I'LL WAKE UP AT: _____

WHAT MEMORABLE MOMENT(S) DID I EXPERIENCE RECENTLY?

_____

_____

BENEFITS I FELT TODAY(CIRCLE):

Feel Happier   More Organized   Fuller Day   Increased Productivity   More Energized   Reduced Stress

(You can always surpass a small goal and feel even BETTER about yourself.)

☀ MY MORNING RITUAL TOMORROW WILL BE: *Completed?*

1. _____ ☐
2. _____ ☐
3. _____ ☐
4. _____ ☐
5. _____ ☐

Day 13

LAST NIGHT I SLEPT AT: _____ & WOKE UP TODAY AT: _____

MY MOST IMPORTANT TASK FOR TODAY IS:

_____

WHAT IS ONE SMALL WAY I CAN IMPROVE MYSELF?

_____

Day 14: **Recommended Podcasts** 🎙️

Sleep With Me Podcast.

The *Sleep With Me* podcast is designed to put you to sleep. They do it with a bedtime story. Yes, you read it right, a bedtime story. Just get in bed, press play and drift off into dreamland. Their description is "A Lulling, Droning, Boring Bedtime Story to Distract Your Racing Mind." It is rated 5 stars and is definitely something to try.

How to get started:

1. Find the podcast "Sleep With Me" and choose an episode to listen to.
2. Download the episode to your phone.
3. Go in airplane mode and play the episode.
4. Set your podcast player to automatically stop after the current episode finishes. You can do this on iOS by hitting the moon icon on the bottom of the podcast page (while an episode is playing) and selecting the time you want it to stop playing.

Sleep With Me
Help falling asleep

"Man should forget his anger before he lies down to sleep."
-Mohandas Gandhi

(If meditation is part of your routine, consider using an app like Headspace or our Meditation Sidekick Journal —————— to help grow it further.)

DATE

Night 13

TONIGHT I'LL SLEEP AT: _____ & TOMORROW I'LL WAKE UP AT: _____

WHAT IS ONE UNIQUE THING ABOUT ME THAT MAKES ME INCREDIBLY SPECIAL?

_____

BENEFITS I FELT TODAY (CIRCLE):

🙂	☰	↑	⊘	♥	🧘
Feel Happier	More Organized	Fuller Day	Increased Productivity	More Energized	Reduced Stress

(If you miss doing your full routine in the mornings, feel free to resume them later in the day.)

MY MORNING RITUAL TOMORROW WILL BE: *Completed?*

1. _____ ☐
2. _____ ☐
3. _____ ☐
4. _____ ☐
5. _____ ☐

Day 14

LAST NIGHT I SLEPT AT: _____ & WOKE UP TODAY AT: _____

MY MOST IMPORTANT TASK FOR TODAY IS:

_____

WHAT IS ONE WAY I AM NOT FULLY LIVING UP TO MY POTENTIAL?

_____

81

Day 15: **Daily Challenge**

Challenge: Determine an activity that'll have you excited about waking up to start the day and insert it into your routine.

If you wake up and dread whatever is ahead of you in the day, it doesn't matter what time you wake up - you'll hate it. When you wake up without excitement, it is hard to even get out of bed.

But if you figure out how to make your mornings exciting – if you wake up and you're like, "I can't wait to get up. This day is going to be awesome. I'm going to do SO MUCH this morning and set an example for not just the rest of my day but the rest of my week and life!" you put yourself in a *beautiful state*. It won't matter how sleep-deprived you may be or what obstacles you have ahead - you'll jump out of bed with an eye looking forward to the beautiful day to come.

Figure out how to make your mornings exciting by choosing what you're excited about the next day. While you're writing down your wake-up time the night before, spend 30 seconds to figure out what you can do to make sure you have the PERFECT start to the day. Maybe it's reading a few pages, meditating, or telling yourself you're going to make today one of the best days of your life.

☐ I completed this daily challenge.

"If you think there aren't enough hours in the day to achieve your dreams, wake up earlier in the morning." - Anonymous

Night 14

TONIGHT I'LL SLEEP AT: _____ & TOMORROW I'LL WAKE UP AT: _____

WHAT IS AN AREA OF WEAKNESS I HAVE IN MY LIFE THAT I WANT TO IMPROVE ON?

_____

BENEFITS I FELT TODAY (CIRCLE):

Feel Happier	More Organized	Fuller Day	Increased Productivity	More Energized	Reduced Stress

MY MORNING RITUAL TOMORROW WILL BE: *Completed?*

1. _____ ☐
2. _____ ☐
3. _____ ☐
4. _____ ☐
5. _____ ☐

Day 15

LAST NIGHT I SLEPT AT: _____ & WOKE UP TODAY AT: _____

MY MOST IMPORTANT TASK FOR TODAY IS:

_____

WHAT IS A CHALLENGE - BIG OR SMALL - I'VE SUCCESSFULLY MOVED PAST TODAY?

_____

Day 16: **Affirmations**

1. Find a quiet area where you can do this in private so you can be at ease. If you can't find a private space, say these in your head while pretending you're screaming them from a mountaintop.

2. Think of a time when you felt absolutely powerful - **when you felt on top of the world**. Tap into every emotion you had at that moment and get yourself into that state right now. How were you feeling then - Powerful? Unstoppable? Strong? Incredible!? Get into it now!!!!

3. Now feel your intensity grow tenfold! Say this with deep passion:

I see how successful people around the world understand that to get what you want in life you have to utilize every single day to its full potential.

I will LEAP out of bed as soon as my alarm goes off at _____ A.M. and begin the day with a surge of energy.

I will use the extra morning time to do some of the best habits known to man.

My productivity, efficiency, and energy will soar through the roof by waking up with purpose and intention.

Repeat this **one more time.**

"The difference between rising at five and seven o'clock in the morning, for forty years, supposing a man to go to bed at the same hour at night, is nearly equivalent to the addition of ten years to a man's life."
- Philip Doddridge

Night 15

TONIGHT I'LL SLEEP AT: _____ & TOMORROW I'LL WAKE UP AT: _____

WHAT IS A SKILL I'VE BUILT IN MY LIFE THAT I USED TO MY BENEFIT TODAY?

_____

BENEFITS I FELT TODAY (CIRCLE):

Feel Happier   More Organized   Fuller Day   Increased Productivity   More Energized   Reduced Stress

MY MORNING RITUAL TOMORROW WILL BE:

Completed?

(If you consistently don't complete your full routine, what can you alter about it?)

1. _____ ☐
2. _____ ☐
3. _____ ☐
4. _____ ☐
5. _____ ☐

Day 16

LAST NIGHT I SLEPT AT: _____ & WOKE UP TODAY AT: _____

MY MOST IMPORTANT TASK FOR TODAY IS:

_____

WHO IS ONE PERSON WHO I CAN GIVE EXTRA CARE AND ATTENTION TO TODAY?

_____

Day 17: **Pro-Tip**

<u>*Become a ninja napper.*</u>

Certain days you will feel tired and drained. It's inevitable, especially if you haven't slept 7-9 hours consistently for the last few days or weeks. Taking 20-minute naps is the most efficient and effective way to boost yourself up with energy. But many of us struggle with naps - specifically with actually falling asleep.

<u>Game-changer:</u> **You don't need to fall asleep to benefit from a nap.**

Letting your mind drift off and relax will restore your body with energy. This 20-minute number has been backed by studies, stating it's the most efficient 'bang for your buck' (for time spent napping to energy gained). Knowing this, you can use it as incentive when you set up a very early wake-up time. As sleep-deprived as you may be getting up then, know you can fill yourself up with energy with quick naps during the day. Use this to push the limits of when you wake up.

<u>How to nap properly</u>:
1. Put your phone in airplane mode.
2. Set a timer on your phone for 20 minutes.
3. Rest your eyes for 20 minutes.
4. Once the 20-minute timer goes off, start moving quickly. Spark yourself with energy so your drowsiness dissipates. If not, you'll transition into the slower sleep cycle, taking 90+ minutes.

"A day without a nap is like a cupcake without frosting."
- Terri Guillemots

Night 16

TONIGHT I'LL SLEEP AT: _____ & TOMORROW I'LL WAKE UP AT: _____

WHAT IS ONE THING I DID TODAY THAT WILL HAVE A CHAIN-EFFECT OF SPREADING POSITIVITY?

_____

⊘ BENEFITS I FELT TODAY (CIRCLE):

Feel Happier More Organized Fuller Day Increased Productivity More Energized Reduced Stress

☀ MY MORNING RITUAL TOMORROW WILL BE: *Completed?*

1. _____ ☐
2. _____ ☐
3. _____ ☐
4. _____ ☐
5. _____ ☐

Day 17

LAST NIGHT I SLEPT AT: _____ & WOKE UP TODAY AT: _____

🐸 MY MOST IMPORTANT TASK FOR TODAY IS:

_____

IF I WERE LIVING AS THE ABSOLUTE BEST VERSION OF MYSELF, WHAT CAN I CHANGE ABOUT MY ACTIONS TODAY?

_____

Day 18: **Recommended Podcast**

The 5 AM Miracle with Jeff Sanders.

 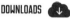
The 5 AM Miracle is a weekly podcast, every Monday, with one objective: to help you dominate your day before breakfast. Jeff Sanders, the host, is dedicated to helping people jump out of bed with enthusiasm, to create lifelong habits, and to tackle big goals with incredible energy.

Although this podcast's title appeals more to early risers, even night owls can learn from some of the lessons of improving their routines.

Waking up with intention, with a plan, and with a solidified purpose can make a dramatic difference in your day, and more importantly, in your future success. Each episode either features a fascinating guest or Jeff himself jumps on the mic and dives into a new topic. The core topics include early mornings, healthy habits, personal development, and rockin' productivity!

Check out his podcast by searching "5AM Miracle" on **any podcasting app like *iTunes*, *iHeart Radio*, *Stitcher*, or *Spreaker*.**

"Morning is an important time of day, because how you spend your morning can often tell you what kind of day you are going to have."
- Lemony Snicket

(Have you been embracing your days of struggle? They're big blessings in disguise as you can learn so much from them.)

Night 17

TONIGHT I'LL SLEEP AT: _____ & TOMORROW I'LL WAKE UP AT: _____

IF A CLOSE FRIEND SAW HOW I HANDLED MY DAY TODAY, WHAT WOULD THEY TELL ME?

_____

BENEFITS I FELT TODAY (CIRCLE):

Feel Happier   More Organized   Fuller Day   Increased Productivity   More Energized   Reduced Stress

MY MORNING RITUAL TOMORROW WILL BE: *Completed?*

1. _____ ☐
2. _____ ☐
3. _____ ☐
4. _____ ☐
5. _____ ☐

Day 18

LAST NIGHT I SLEPT AT: _____ & WOKE UP TODAY AT: _____

MY MOST IMPORTANT TASK FOR TODAY IS:

_____

WHAT CAUSES ME STRESS AND HOW COULD I BETTER RESPOND TO IT?

_____

Day 19: **Pro-Tip**

Use grayscale mode on your phone to break a phone addiction.

After a long day - when we're tired at night and just want to relax - it's so easy to turn to our phones for easy entertainment.

This is totally fine, though sometimes this habit can get out of line and become more destructive than it is pleasant.

One incredibly useful tip has been to put your phone into grayscale mode so that everything is black and white. This may sound simple, but by breaking the visual hook of color, your phone loses that irresistible "I just can't put this down" element. Some people even incorporate this into their nighttime routine each night before bed.

On an iPhone, you can set this as your accessibility shortcut so when you **triple tap the home button** (or the power button for iPhone X users or later) it automatically switches from color to grayscale. Set this up in: _Settings > General > Accessibility > Color Filters._

Due to the variety of Android phones / software adoption, using Google is your best bet for finding the specific steps to do this.

GRAYSCALE ON!

"Every day may not be good, but there's something good in every day"
-Alice Morse Earle

90

Night 18

TONIGHT I'LL SLEEP AT: _____ & TOMORROW I'LL WAKE UP AT: _____

WHAT AM I GREAT AT THAT I DON'T GIVE MYSELF ENOUGH CREDIT FOR?

_____

BENEFITS I FELT TODAY (CIRCLE):

Feel Happier   More Organized   Fuller Day   Increased Productivity   More Energized   Reduced Stress

MY MORNING RITUAL TOMORROW WILL BE: *Completed?*

1. _____ ☐
2. _____ ☐
3. _____ ☐
4. _____ ☐
5. _____ ☐

Day 19

LAST NIGHT I SLEPT AT: _____ & WOKE UP TODAY AT: _____

MY MOST IMPORTANT TASK FOR TODAY IS:

_____

IF I WERE TO MAKE NO EXCUSES FOR MY LIFE, WHAT WOULD I DO DIFFERENTLY?

_____

Day 20: **Affirmations**

1. Find a quiet area where you can do this in private so you can be at ease. If you can't find a private space, say these in your head while pretending you're screaming them from a mountaintop.

2. Think of a time when you felt absolutely powerful - **when you felt on top of the world**. Tap into every emotion you had at that moment and get yourself into that state right now. How were you feeling then - Powerful? Unstoppable? Strong? Incredible!? Get into it now!!!!

3. Now feel your intensity grow tenfold! Say this with deep passion:

By taking good care of my body with the extra time I have in the morning, I feel accomplished, vibrant, energetic, and healthy throughout the day.

I am no longer negatively affected by the needs of my body because I wake up on time and make sure I feel empowered so that I can accomplish everything I set out to do.

Repeat this **one more time.**

"Dreaming or doing is a choice that will mean the difference between failure and success."
-Anonymous

Night 19

TONIGHT I'LL SLEEP AT: _____ & TOMORROW I'LL WAKE UP AT: _____

HOW HAVE I POSITIVELY IMPACTED SOMEONE'S LIFE TODAY?

_____

BENEFITS I FELT TODAY (CIRCLE):

| Feel Happier | More Organized | Fuller Day | Increased Productivity | More Energized | Reduced Stress |

MY MORNING RITUAL TOMORROW WILL BE: *Completed?*

1. _____ ☐
2. _____ ☐
3. _____ ☐
4. _____ ☐
5. _____ ☐

Day 20

LAST NIGHT I SLEPT AT: _____ & WOKE UP TODAY AT: _____

MY MOST IMPORTANT TASK FOR TODAY IS:

_____

WHAT IS ONE SMALL WAY I CAN IMPROVE MYSELF?

_____

Day 21: **Success Story**

Benjamin Franklin.

Benjamin Franklin is, of course, one of the founding fathers of the United States. What you probably don't know is that he's also the founding father of the 'to-do list.'

He had some specific rules for how he started each morning. His three-hour block of morning routine stretched from 5:00 A.M. to 8:00 A.M. and included addressing "Powerful Goodness" and setting a plan for the rest of his day.

Every morning he asked himself, "What good shall I do today?"

See if any of his routines are useful for you to adopt. You can also experiment with planning your day out in the extreme hour-by-hour detail like Franklin did below:

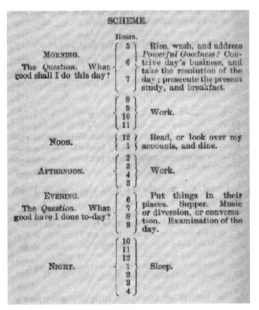

"Genius is 1% talent and 99% hard work." - Albert Einstein

TONIGHT I'LL SLEEP AT: _____ & TOMORROW I'LL WAKE UP AT: _____

Night 20

WHAT IS SOMETHING I SPENT TIME ON TODAY THAT COULD POSITIVELY IMPACT MY FUTURE?

_____

BENEFITS I FELT TODAY (CIRCLE):

Feel Happier   More Organized   Fuller Day   Increased Productivity   More Energized   Reduced Stress

MY MORNING RITUAL TOMORROW WILL BE:

Completed?

1. _____ ☐
2. _____ ☐
3. _____ ☐
4. _____ ☐
5. _____ ☐

Day 21

LAST NIGHT I SLEPT AT: _____ & WOKE UP TODAY AT: _____

MY MOST IMPORTANT TASK FOR TODAY IS:

_____

WHERE IS ONE PLACE I AM SPENDING TIME THAT DOES NOT BRING ME REAL HAPPINESS?

_____

PHASE 2.

DESTROYED.

Note: We LOVE sharing stories of our users and what their lives looked like BEFORE using the journal compared to where they are NOW!

If you want to share your story with us, you can do so here:
habitnest.com/morningtestimonial

Phase 2 Recap: Days 8-21

1. What have you realized to be the most important elements for you to have a productive morning and day?

_____

_____

2. What nighttime habits should you be doing consistently?

_____

_____

3. What are some new rituals you want to experiment with?

_____

_____

4. How has being laser-focused about your mornings impacted your life?

_____

_____

_____

5. How would you feel if you stopped doing this?

_____

_____

_____

PHASE 3:

DAYS 22-66+

 ~~Phase 1~~   ~~Phase 2~~   **Phase 3**

| ~~Days 01-07~~ | ~~Days 08-21~~ | **Days 22-66+** |
| ~~Hell Week.~~ | ~~Staying Consistent.~~ | **Rewiring Your Brain.** |

Phase 3: Hardwiring - Retaining Interest In Your Personal Improvement

Congratulations, you've made it to Phase 3. You've shown serious commitment to the incredible future you envision for yourself!

This is a great phase to explore how to make the most out of this habit for you, personally. Most people use this phase to experiment with different routines, wake-up times, hours of sleep, etc. to tweak what works for them.

It's easy to take the benefits you're feeling for granted — it's extremely easy to fall off the wagon, especially in this phase.

Keep going strong until having the best mornings of your life is engrained in your DNA.

This means pushing through to stick with your commitments on your best days, your worst days, and especially the days where you just don't feel like it (those are the *most important*).

Commit.

I am INCREDIBLE.

I've come a long way,
but the road doesn't end here.

It's time to ingrain this habit in me forever.

I will see this
huge challenge all the way through.

Mastering this habit is only the
beginning of my perpetual growth.

_____

Nothing will stop me now.

_____   _____
Signature   Date

Phase 2 Medal
Earned!

Day 22: **Pro-Tip**

Get to know your body clock.

It's weird to think that most of us don't know how much sleep our body naturally needs because we either sleep too late or sleep too much.

1. Stick to sleeping at a normal hour for a week straight (somewhere from 9:00 P.M. to 11 P.M.).

2. Allow your body to wake up without disturbance – no snoozing, no going back to sleep after you wake up. This will give you a better sense of how much sleep your body wants as opposed to how much sleep your mind wants (oftentimes we 'think' we need more sleep than we actually do).

3. Based on how much sleep you find your body needs, you can properly make decisions about when to sleep, which should be based on exactly when you want to get up in the morning.

"And when you find out what your WHY is – and your WHY gotta be deeper than you – When you find your WHY. You don't hit snooze no more! When you find your WHY. You find a way to make it happen!"
- Eric Thomas

102

Night 21

TONIGHT I'LL SLEEP AT: _____ & TOMORROW I'LL WAKE UP AT: _____

WHAT MEMORABLE MOMENT(S) DID I EXPERIENCE RECENTLY?

_____

OPENING UP ABOUT MY DAY:

_____

_____

_____

MY MORNING RITUAL TOMORROW WILL BE: *Completed?*

1. _____ ☐
2. _____ ☐
3. _____ ☐
4. _____ ☐
5. _____ ☐

Day 22

LAST NIGHT I SLEPT AT: _____ & WOKE UP TODAY AT: _____

MY MOST IMPORTANT TASK FOR TODAY IS:

_____

**WHAT IS ONE TIME I WANT TO BE MORE PRESENT
AND LESS DISTRACTED DURING MY DAY?**

_____

Day 23: **Daily Challenge** ◊

Challenge: Take action on something that you know will make you
want to cringe because it falls outside the walls of your comfort zone.

Begin to notice the comfort zone you've created for yourself. You'll
realize that the little world you're living in LIMITS you in every
possible way. To grow, you must break through these artificial limits.

We all have a comfort zone. Our comfort zone is who we are - things
we're willing to deal with, activities we're willing engage in, people
we're willing to create relationships with, etc.

The difference between you and anyone else is self-created
limitations - some have bigger, more generous comfort zones, and
some live in a very small world. Regardless of the size of your
comfort zone, it's your biggest enemy. Comfort zones prevent us
from taking action!

*Nobody ever grows in a comfort zone. **Ever**.*

We love our comfort zones because **we're afraid of failure, afraid of
rejection, but most of all, afraid to disappoint ourselves** - by our
own definition of what disappointment is. Your definition of
disappointment is completely BS and quite frankly nobody cares if
you succeed or fail. **Don't be afraid of looking vulnerable.** Take
massive action and show yourself what's truly possible.

☐ I completed this daily challenge.

WHERE GREATNESS
HAPPENS

YOUR
COMFORT→ 🧍
ZONE

Night 22

DATE _____

TONIGHT I'LL SLEEP AT: _____ & TOMORROW I'LL WAKE UP AT: _____

WHAT IS ONE EMOTIONAL RESPONSE I HAD TODAY THAT I AM PROUD OF?

_____

(This new section is designed to be your open canvas for any writing, reflecting, or creative thinking!)

OPENING UP ABOUT MY DAY:

_____
_____
_____

MY MORNING RITUAL TOMORROW WILL BE: *Completed?*

1. _____ ☐
2. _____ ☐
3. _____ ☐
4. _____ ☐
5. _____ ☐

Day 23

LAST NIGHT I SLEPT AT: _____ & WOKE UP TODAY AT: _____

MY MOST IMPORTANT TASK FOR TODAY IS:

_____

WHEN WAS THE LAST TIME I DID NOT STICK TO MY WORD? HOW CAN I AVOID DOING SO AGAIN?

_____

105

Day 24: **Affirmations**

1. Find a quiet area where you can do this in private so you can be at ease. If you can't find a private space, say these in your head while pretending you're screaming them from a mountaintop.

2. Think of a time when you felt absolutely powerful - **when you felt on top of the world**. Tap into every emotion you had at that moment and get yourself into that state right now. How were you feeling then - Powerful? Unstoppable? Strong? Incredible!? Get into it now!!!!

3. Now feel your intensity grow tenfold! Say this with deep passion:

I am fulfilling my life's mission to master my mornings and boosting the quality of my entire day. I will stop at nothing to make this a reality for myself. My life will reach a whole new level it's never seen before!

I am fulfilling my mission of having the most productive days of my life. The extra time I receive from being laser-focused when I wake up gives me a secret edge to conquer my day.

Repeat this **one more time.**

EVERY PASSING DAY
IT BECOMES EASIER
AND EASIER
TO WAKE UP EARLY

"Affirmations are like seed planted in soil. Poor soil, poor growth. Rich soil, abundant growth. The more you choose to think thoughts that make you feel good, the quicker the affirmations work." - Louise L. Hay

TONIGHT I'LL SLEEP AT: _____ & TOMORROW I'LL WAKE UP AT: _____

Night 23

HOW HAS MY OUTLOOK ON LIFE IMPROVED MY DAY?

_____

(Some people use this to think of ways to improve this habit in the long-run. Others to reflect on their days.)

OPENING UP ABOUT MY DAY:

_____
_____
_____

MY MORNING RITUAL TOMORROW WILL BE: *Completed?*

1. _____ ☐
2. _____ ☐
3. _____ ☐
4. _____ ☐
5. _____ ☐

Day 24

LAST NIGHT I SLEPT AT: _____ & WOKE UP TODAY AT: _____

MY MOST IMPORTANT TASK FOR TODAY IS:

_____

WHAT IS ONE AREA I CAN APPROACH WITH MORE ENTHUSIASM AND ENERGY TODAY?

_____

Day 25: **Super Read**

Amazon Reviews: 192

★★★★★ 4.3

Title: _Wake Up Successful - How to Increase Your Energy and Achieve Any Goal with a Morning Routine_
Author: S.J. Scott

First of all, S.J. Scott is one of the most active authors in the personal development space with tons of incredible content. This is one of his many books, jam-packed with strategies, tips, routines, examples, and suggested rituals. In fact, we used his _Master Evernote_ book to organize a lot of our notes in compiling this journal.

In _Wake Up Successful_ you'll learn how to live every day like it's your last. No longer will you stumble out of bed and waste the first few hours. Instead, you'll learn how to start the day by creating energy and using this power to focus on ONE breakthrough goal that will make a difference in your life.

A morning routine is simple and effective. It's easy to tailor to your unique goals. And, best of all, it's tested. Inside this book, you'll discover the proven strategies to help you get the most out of those precious first few hours.

"Simply wake up every morning a better person than when [you] went to bed." - Sidney Poitier

TONIGHT I'LL SLEEP AT: _____ & TOMORROW I'LL WAKE UP AT: _____

Night 24

🤝 HOW HAVE I SET MY FUTURE SELF UP FOR SUCCESS TODAY?

_____

(Idea: Use
this as a
place to
write out a
nighttime
routine for
yourself.)

✏️ OPENING UP ABOUT MY DAY:

_____

_____

_____

☀️ MY MORNING RITUAL TOMORROW WILL BE: *Completed?*

1. _____ ☐
2. _____ ☐
3. _____ ☐
4. _____ ☐
5. _____ ☐

Day 25

LAST NIGHT I SLEPT AT: _____ & WOKE UP TODAY AT: _____

🐸 MY MOST IMPORTANT TASK FOR TODAY IS:

_____

⊕ WHO IS SOMEONE THAT WILL HAVE A POSITIVE EFFECT IN MY LIFE THAT I SHOULD SPEND MORE TIME WITH?

_____

Day 26: **Daily Challenge**

**Challenge: Maintain consistency throughout the weekend.**

On the weekend, we have a completely different schedule than during the rest of the week. We sleep late, we do completely different tasks. The problem is - your body doesn't know that. To your body, Monday morning and Sunday morning are the same exact thing.

If you're waking up at 5 A.M. throughout the week and then begin sleeping very late on the weekends, you'll confuse your body and your system. From this inconsistency, it's going to be much harder for you to start waking up as planned in upcoming weekdays.

If waking up at the same time on weekends means you become a bit sleep deprived, it is oftentimes worth it. You can make up for it with napping in the day. Plus the benefit of remaining consistent will carry on throughout the upcoming days, weeks, and months ahead.

For the sake of consistency, treat weekends and weekdays the same. Attempt making weekdays and weekends follow the same routine – at least for 1 week straight.

☐ I completed this daily challenge.

SATURDAY 7AM

"For the past 33 years, I have looked in the mirror every morning and asked myself: 'If today were the last day of my life, would I want to do what I am about to do today?'
And whenever the answer has been no for too many days in a row, I know I need to change something." - Steve Jobs

TONIGHT I'LL SLEEP AT: _____ & TOMORROW I'LL WAKE UP AT: _____

Night 25

HOW HAVE I SHOWN SELF-LOVE AND CARE TO MYSELF TODAY?

_____

✏ OPENING UP ABOUT MY DAY:

(Idea: write about this prompt: "Who did I help in the world today and how?")

_____

_____

_____

☀ MY MORNING RITUAL TOMORROW WILL BE: *Completed?*

(Feel free to experiment with new rituals as you advance through this habit.)

1. _____ ☐

2. _____ ☐

3. _____ ☐

4. _____ ☐

5. _____ ☐

Day 26

LAST NIGHT I SLEPT AT: _____ & WOKE UP TODAY AT: _____

🐸 MY MOST IMPORTANT TASK FOR TODAY IS:

_____

WHAT IS ONE SMALL WAY I CAN IMPROVE MYSELF?

_____

Day 27: **Recommended Podcast**
The Chalene Show with Chalene Johnson.

Chalene Johnson is a health expert and entrepreneur. Her personable yet straightforward approach to living a better life has gotten her podcast *The Chalene Show* to a 5 star rating after 4000 reviews!

Stated in her bio, several years ago, Chalene began to suffer a steady decline in her health that included debilitating brain fog, mood swings, and chronic pain and injuries. This led her to question the diet and fitness industries' definition of health, and subsequently transitioned her focus from business to health and wellness. She taught herself to read scientific studies, as well as how to search for, find, question, and evaluate research.

The Chalene Show explores the intersection between health, lifestyle, and living a fulfilled life all with a down-to-earth, practical approach.

She talks about her experience with becoming a morning person with suggestions and tips on Episode 261, *How to become a Morning Person.*

To check out her podcast, search for: *The Chalene Show* on **any podcasting app like *iTunes, iHeart Radio, Stitcher,* or *Spreaker.***

"Eating right and taking the time to slow down and plan in the morning is crucial to a productive day." – David Moore

TONIGHT I'LL SLEEP AT: _____ & TOMORROW I'LL WAKE UP AT: _____

Night 26

WHAT MEMORABLE MOMENT(S) DID I EXPERIENCE RECENTLY?

OPENING UP ABOUT MY DAY:

To test new
habits you're
interested
in, you
could give
yourself a
mini "3-day
challenge" to
see if you
like them.)

☀ MY MORNING RITUAL TOMORROW WILL BE: *Completed?*

1. _____ ☐

2. _____ ☐

3. _____ ☐

4. _____ ☐

5. _____ ☐

Day 27

LAST NIGHT I SLEPT AT: _____ & WOKE UP TODAY AT: _____

MY MOST IMPORTANT TASK FOR TODAY IS:

WHAT IS ONE WAY I AM NOT FULLY LIVING UP TO MY POTENTIAL?

Day 28: **Affirmations**

1. Find a quiet area where you can do this in private so you can be at ease. If you can't find a private space, say these in your head while pretending you're screaming them from a mountaintop.

2. Think of a time when you felt absolutely powerful - **when you felt on top of the world**. Tap into every emotion you had at that moment and get yourself into that state right now. How were you feeling then - Powerful? Unstoppable? Strong? Incredible!? Get into it now!!!!

3. Now feel your intensity grow tenfold! Say this with deep passion:

Every day I do my morning routine, I attract beauty, sparks of fun, and surges of happiness to my life. The more I own my mornings, the more pure goodness will flow into my life effortlessly.

By mastering myself and my life, I skyrocket the quality of my life. My passion deeply outweighs any of the challenges I will face on this journey. I own this. I can do this, I can do this easily, and I can do this now.

Repeat this **one more time.**

I WAKE UP EARLY AND MAKE SURE I FEEL PERFECT
SO THAT I CAN ACCOMPLISH EVERYTHING I SET OUT TO DO

Night 27

TONIGHT I'LL SLEEP AT: _____ & TOMORROW I'LL WAKE UP AT: _____

**WHAT IS ONE UNIQUE THING ABOUT ME
THAT MAKES ME INCREDIBLY SPECIAL?**

_____

(You can
also use this
space to
record the
benefits
you're
feeling
about your
journey,
similar to
Phase 2.)

OPENING UP ABOUT MY DAY:

_____

_____

_____

MY MORNING RITUAL TOMORROW WILL BE: _Completed?_

1. _____ ☐
2. _____ ☐
3. _____ ☐
4. _____ ☐
5. _____ ☐

Day 28

LAST NIGHT I SLEPT AT: _____ & WOKE UP TODAY AT: _____

MY MOST IMPORTANT TASK FOR TODAY IS:

_____

**WHAT IS AN AREA OF WEAKNESS I HAVE IN
MY LIFE THAT I WANT TO IMPROVE ON?**

_____

Day 29: **Favorite Resources**

Product: Sleep Cycle™ (iPhone or Android App).
Cost: $0.99.
Note: We have no affiliation with Sleep Cycle™. We just love the app.

Feeling fresh the moment you open your eyes is all about timing. The Sleep Cycle™ alarm clock tracks your sleep patterns and wakes you up when you're in a light sleep state. Waking up during light sleep feels like waking up naturally rested without an alarm clock — it's a pretty amazing feeling, and the app works surprisingly accurately too.

1. You go through phases when you sleep (first light sleep, then deep sleep, then Rapid Eye Movement sleep) and your movements in sleep vary with each phase.
2. The app tracks your movements (or sounds) to wake you up during the light phase of your sleep using a 30 minute alarm window of your choice.
3. Your sleep patterns are tracked on a graph to show you at what points in the night you are in either light, deep or REM sleep.

Download: www.sleepcycle.com

"I get up every morning and it's going to be a great day. You never know when it's going to be over so I refuse to have a bad day."
- Paul Henderson

TONIGHT I'LL SLEEP AT: _____ & TOMORROW I'LL WAKE UP AT: _____

Night 28

WHAT IS A CHALLENGE - BIG OR SMALL - I'VE SUCCESSFULLY MOVED PAST TODAY?

_____

OPENING UP ABOUT MY DAY:

_____

_____

_____

MY MORNING RITUAL TOMORROW WILL BE:

Completed?

1. _____ ☐
2. _____ ☐
3. _____ ☐
4. _____ ☐
5. _____ ☐

Day 29

LAST NIGHT I SLEPT AT: _____ & WOKE UP TODAY AT: _____

MY MOST IMPORTANT TASK FOR TODAY IS:

_____

WHO IS ONE PERSON WHO I CAN GIVE EXTRA CARE AND ATTENTION TO TODAY?

_____

Day 30: **User Success Story**

Karen N., Morning Sidekick Journal User
Karen's biggest challenge when it came to changing her morning routine:

"I felt like I was a failure if I didn't get everything on my list done (a list longer than the D.C. phonebook).

I have post traumatic stress from a difficult childhood. Any project I ever began would never be quite finished. In that way I would perpetuate the self loathing I brought with me in to my adult life. The *Morning Sidekick Journal* is a tool you can use for accountability, but in a way that you are not chastised for not doing this 'perfectly'. It actually tells you the expectation is that it won't be perfect. You get support with the journal."

Karen challenges other Morning Sidekick Journal users to:

"For those Morning Sidekick journalers such as myself that are dealing with mental illness, depression, substance abuse, or any other form of recovery, you can adapt this to any type of program you are on. I don't work a regular schedule and only use the journal four days a week - for home use. Others will need to adapt it to the days they are working and maybe not on their days off. Others may be able to use the journal every day of the week. The point here is there is no single way of doing it - you can adapt it to every lifestyle. Every way is the 'right way'. No longer a failure - you are now a work in progress. Come up with a way you can adapt and use the *Morning Sidekick Journal* to best fit your specific needs."

TONIGHT I'LL SLEEP AT: _____ & TOMORROW I'LL WAKE UP AT: _____

Night 29

WHAT IS A SKILL I'VE BUILT IN MY LIFE THAT I USED TO MY BENEFIT TODAY?

_____

OPENING UP ABOUT MY DAY:

_____

_____

_____

MY MORNING RITUAL TOMORROW WILL BE:

Completed?

1. _____ ☐
2. _____ ☐
3. _____ ☐
4. _____ ☐
5. _____ ☐

Day 30

LAST NIGHT I SLEPT AT: _____ & WOKE UP TODAY AT: _____

MY MOST IMPORTANT TASK FOR TODAY IS:

_____

IF I WERE LIVING AS THE ABSOLUTE BEST VERSION OF MYSELF, WHAT CAN I CHANGE ABOUT MY ACTIONS TODAY?

_____

Day 31: **Affirmations**

1. Find a quiet area where you can do this in private so you can be at ease. If you can't find a private space, say these in your head while pretending you're screaming them from a mountaintop.

2. Think of a time when you felt absolutely powerful - **when you felt on top of the world**. Tap into every emotion you had at that moment and get yourself into that state right now. How were you feeling then - Powerful? Unstoppable? Strong? Incredible!? Get into it now!!!!

3. Now feel your intensity grow tenfold! Say this with deep passion:

I will wake up on time every day no matter how hard it is. I will wake up full of energy and purpose as soon as I hear the sound of my alarm.

Because I wake up when planned and jump into my morning routine, I serve as a shining example who inspires others to conquer their mornings.

Repeat this **one more time**.

"I used to love night best but the older I get the more treasures and hope and joy I find in mornings." - Terri Guillemots

TONIGHT I'LL SLEEP AT: _____ & TOMORROW I'LL WAKE UP AT: _____

Night 30

WHAT IS ONE THING I DID TODAY THAT WILL HAVE A CHAIN-EFFECT OF SPREADING POSITIVITY?

_____

OPENING UP ABOUT MY DAY:

_____

_____

_____

MY MORNING RITUAL TOMORROW WILL BE: _Completed?_

1. _____ ☐

2. _____ ☐

3. _____ ☐

4. _____ ☐

5. _____ ☐

Day 31

LAST NIGHT I SLEPT AT: _____ & WOKE UP TODAY AT: _____

MY MOST IMPORTANT TASK FOR TODAY IS:

_____

WHAT CAUSES ME STRESS AND HOW COULD I BETTER RESPOND TO IT?

_____

Day 32: **Pro-Tip**

Write down your desired wake-up time.

Reading that above statement, you may wonder how this will help you wake up when planned. The simple fact is, that writing down the time you want to wake up makes your goal tangible and REAL for you. It creates a physical expectation of yourself that's now written out into the world (instead of just staying in your mind). This makes it harder for you to break it.

When you write down what time you want to wake up the night before, you better internalize the information/goal. Your mindset switches a little bit. The night before, just write down on a piece of paper, "I want to wake up at…" and fill in the blank - whether it's 5, 8, or 11 A.M. **Write it down.** It's going to be better ingrained in your brain; your mindset is going to be different.

When it's dark outside, you're waking up, and all the voices in your head are saying, "Don't wake up, go back to bed," you need to use every piece of ammunition you have.

"I usually get up at 5 or 5:15am….I am not a big sleeper and never have been. Life is too exciting to sleep." - Howard Schultz

Night 31

TONIGHT I'LL SLEEP AT: _____ & TOMORROW I'LL WAKE UP AT: _____

 IF A CLOSE FRIEND SAW HOW I HANDLED MY DAY TODAY, WHAT WOULD THEY TELL ME?

_____

 OPENING UP ABOUT MY DAY:

_____

_____

_____

MY MORNING RITUAL TOMORROW WILL BE: *Completed?*

1. _____ ☐
2. _____ ☐
3. _____ ☐
4. _____ ☐
5. _____ ☐

Day 32

LAST NIGHT I SLEPT AT: _____ & WOKE UP TODAY AT: _____

MY MOST IMPORTANT TASK FOR TODAY IS:

_____

IF I WERE TO MAKE NO EXCUSES FOR MY LIFE, WHAT WOULD I DO DIFFERENTLY?

_____

123

Day 33: **Daily Challenge** 🔥

Challenge: Build the habit of shifting between 'off' and 'on' days.

As we covered before, it's very common to have failed and missed days as you grow a morning routine in your life. One critical value point we hope you take away from this experience is building the habit of **moving FROM a point of failure** (missing a day or multiple days) **BACK to the effort of rebuilding this habit.**

That is where the magic happens.

Arguably, missing days make up a critical component of being realistic that you likely won't wake up at 5am every day for the rest of your life, yet that whenever you want to, you can call back on your ability to SHIFT BACK into that habit.

That is what this journal will provide you - the ability to choose and call upon this habit whenever and however often you'd like.

Action step: The next time you fail, remind yourself the immense long-term value of getting back on track and rebuilding that skill.

"Let today be the day you give up who you've been for who you can become." - Hal Elrod

Night 32

TONIGHT I'LL SLEEP AT: _____ & TOMORROW I'LL WAKE UP AT: _____

WHAT AM I GREAT AT THAT I DON'T GIVE MYSELF ENOUGH CREDIT FOR?

_____

OPENING UP ABOUT MY DAY:

_____

_____

_____

MY MORNING RITUAL TOMORROW WILL BE: *Completed?*

1. _____ ☐
2. _____ ☐
3. _____ ☐
4. _____ ☐
5. _____ ☐

Day 33

LAST NIGHT I SLEPT AT: _____ & WOKE UP TODAY AT: _____

MY MOST IMPORTANT TASK FOR TODAY IS:

_____

**WHERE IS ONE PLACE I AM SPENDING TIME THAT
DOES NOT BRING ME REAL HAPPINESS?**

_____

Day 34: **Success Story**

Bob Iger, Disney™ CEO.

Iger gets up at 4:30 every morning. He takes the quiet time to do a number of things together, such as reading the papers, exercising, listening to music, looking at email, and watching TV all at the same time. This CEO is multitasking before the sun comes out.

He said in order to keep the company pushing out some of the greatest films he has to wake up at 4:30 A.M. From there he's off to the gym at 5, and at the office by 6. For Iger, it's really about re-charging his batteries and clearing his mind.

"I get up at 4:30 in the morning, seven days a week, no matter where I am in the world." - Bob Iger

Iger does a lot with his mornings - but the most impressive piece is just how consistent he is, waking up at 4:30 A.M. even when traveling. Qualities like this are why he's able to successfully run such a huge, yet magical, corporation.

"Think in the morning. Act in the noon. Eat in the evening. Sleep in the night." - William Blake

Night 33

TONIGHT I'LL SLEEP AT: _____ & TOMORROW I'LL WAKE UP AT: _____

HOW HAVE I POSITIVELY IMPACTED SOMEONE'S LIFE TODAY?

_____

OPENING UP ABOUT MY DAY:

_____

_____

_____

MY MORNING RITUAL TOMORROW WILL BE: *Completed?*

(3-day challenge idea: Meditate for 3 minutes a day.)

1. _____ ☐
2. _____ ☐
3. _____ ☐
4. _____ ☐
5. _____ ☐

Day 34

LAST NIGHT I SLEPT AT: _____ & WOKE UP TODAY AT: _____

MY MOST IMPORTANT TASK FOR TODAY IS:

_____

WHO IS ONE CONTENT CREATOR OR AUTHOR I CAN REVISIT OR LEARN MORE FROM TO IMPROVE MY LIFE?

_____

Day 35: **Affirmations**

1. Find a quiet area where you can do this in private so you can be at ease. If you can't find a private space, say these in your head while pretending you're screaming them from a mountaintop.

2. Think of a time when you felt absolutely powerful - **when you felt on top of the world**. Tap into every emotion you had at that moment and get yourself into that state right now. How were you feeling then - Powerful? Unstoppable? Strong? Incredible!? Get into it now!!!!

3. Now feel your intensity grow tenfold! Say this with deep passion:

By waking up on time, I can knock out my biggest, most important, life-changing tasks of the day early on. By knocking out big tasks early on, I create positive momentum that fuels me for the day.

All this fills me up with mental clarity and peace of mind every day, which in turn helps me master every area of my life.

Repeat this **one more time.**

"Life is waking up an hour early to live an hour more."
- Anonymous

128

Night 34

TONIGHT I'LL SLEEP AT: _____ & TOMORROW I'LL WAKE UP AT: _____

WHAT IS SOMETHING I SPENT TIME ON TODAY THAT COULD POSITIVELY IMPACT MY FUTURE?

_____

OPENING UP ABOUT MY DAY:

_____

_____

_____

MY MORNING RITUAL TOMORROW WILL BE: *Completed?*

1. _____ ☐
2. _____ ☐
3. _____ ☐
4. _____ ☐
5. _____ ☐

Day 35

LAST NIGHT I SLEPT AT: _____ & WOKE UP TODAY AT: _____

MY MOST IMPORTANT TASK FOR TODAY IS:

_____

WHAT IS ONE TIME I WANT TO BE MORE PRESENT AND LESS DISTRACTED DURING MY DAY?

_____

Day 36: **Success Story**

John Paul DeJoria, Co-founder of Patron™

DeJoria begins every single morning, no matter where and when, with about five minutes of quiet reflection to "just be." He spends the time being grateful for what he has.

Immediately after he gathers himself, DeJoria begins his day by checking his calendar for the day and knocking out important phone calls and meetings. The co-founder of Patron™ surprisingly "doesn't do email." He was quoted saying, "I know, I've been told I'm a bit old school, but it all gets done just the way I need it to. It allows me to focus on the important things that need my attention."

Can you incorporate gratitude or writing into your morning routine? Or perhaps spend some time to organize what tasks you will tackle each day and in what order.

"The time just before dawn contains the most energy of all hours of the day. This has helped me become an early riser and an early doer...When I wake to see that it's light out already, I feel the world has started without me." - Terri Guillemets

TONIGHT I'LL SLEEP AT: _____ & TOMORROW I'LL WAKE UP AT: _____

Night 35

WHAT IS ONE EMOTIONAL RESPONSE I HAD TODAY THAT I AM PROUD OF?

_____

OPENING UP ABOUT MY DAY:

_____

_____

_____

MY MORNING RITUAL TOMORROW WILL BE: *Completed?*

1. _____ ☐

2. _____ ☐

3. _____ ☐

4. _____ ☐

5. _____ ☐

Day 36

LAST NIGHT I SLEPT AT: _____ & WOKE UP TODAY AT: _____

MY MOST IMPORTANT TASK FOR TODAY IS:

_____

WHEN WAS THE LAST TIME I DID NOT STICK TO MY WORD?
HOW CAN I AVOID DOING SO AGAIN?

_____

Day 37: **Daily Challenge** 🔥

Challenge: Think about what the image of perfection you've created for yourself is… Now realize that you may NEVER fit that image! Instead, be yourself and love yourself for all that you are.

Most of us subconsciously judge ourselves for not fitting this image of perfection whenever we slip up or struggle even the slightest bit. This is a horrendous activity that will lead you to unhappiness, a spiral of guilt, a feeling of unworthiness, and freeze you in inactivity.

What does this cycle do to help you succeed and live a happy life? **NOTHING.** The truth is, the quicker you can do the following, the happier your life will be day after day.

Anytime you feel you're not in a state of pure happiness:

1. Determine what mistakes you made and what went wrong.
2. Identify what you can learn from this and apply it to your future.
3. **Forgive yourself.** Now forgive yourself again.
4. Love yourself for exactly what you are right now.
5. Now **move forward full-speed ahead** with what you've learned.

It doesn't matter if it takes you 50 learning cycles or 5 years of mistakes — the second you lose is when you throw on that useless guilt and unnecessary negative emotions because you're trashing your quality of life… and increasing your quality of life is the whole point you're doing this all in the first place!

I completed this daily challenge.

Night 36

TONIGHT I'LL SLEEP AT: _____ & TOMORROW I'LL WAKE UP AT: _____

🤝 HOW HAS MY OUTLOOK ON LIFE IMPROVED MY DAY?

_____

✏️ OPENING UP ABOUT MY DAY:

_____

_____

_____

☀️ MY MORNING RITUAL TOMORROW WILL BE: *Completed?*

1. _____ ☐
2. _____ ☐
3. _____ ☐
4. _____ ☐
5. _____ ☐

Day 37

LAST NIGHT I SLEPT AT: _____ & WOKE UP TODAY AT: _____

🏇 MY MOST IMPORTANT TASK FOR TODAY IS:

_____

⊕ WHAT IS ONE AREA I CAN APPROACH WITH MORE ENTHUSIASM AND ENERGY TODAY?

_____

Day 38: **Recommended Podcast** 🎙

<u>The Better Than Happy Podcast by Jody Moore.</u>

Jody is a mother of four and is on a mission to figure out how to minimize resentment, overwhelm, and guilt, and to replace them with happiness, gratitude, and joy.

She delves into maneuvering the different emotions we experience and breaks down WHY we feel that way. She spends a lot of time on exploring mindsets we embody in our lives and how they influence our lives.

Jody does a great job at braking down our relationships with ourselves and does so with a down-to-earth, easy-to-follow approach.

Check out her podcast by searching "Better Than Happy" on **any podcasting app like *iTunes, iHeart Radio, Stitcher*, or *Spreaker*.**

"A dream doesn't become reality through magic: it takes sweat, determination and hard work. The price of success is hard work, dedication to the job at hand, and the determination that whether we win or lose, we have applied the best of ourselves to the task at hand."
- Vince Lombardi

Night 37

TONIGHT I'LL SLEEP AT: _____ & TOMORROW I'LL WAKE UP AT: _____

HOW HAVE I SET MY FUTURE SELF UP FOR SUCCESS TODAY?

_____

OPENING UP ABOUT MY DAY:

_____
_____
_____

MY MORNING RITUAL TOMORROW WILL BE:

Completed?

1. _____ ☐
2. _____ ☐
3. _____ ☐
4. _____ ☐
5. _____ ☐

Day 38

LAST NIGHT I SLEPT AT: _____ & WOKE UP TODAY AT: _____

MY MOST IMPORTANT TASK FOR TODAY IS:

_____

WHO IS SOMEONE THAT WILL HAVE A POSITIVE EFFECT IN MY LIFE THAT I SHOULD SPEND MORE TIME WITH?

_____

Day 39: **Pro-Tip**

Put your phone/alarm away from your bed to force you to get up.

Put your alarm clock or phone (if you use it as an alarm clock) far away from your bed. In the mornings, one of the most crucial steps to getting going is simply stepping out of bed. Getting up to turn off your alarm is a no-brainer solution.

In the mornings, the second you get to your phone to turn off your alarm, do NOT allow yourself to even touch your bed again. Keep moving and go to the bathroom to brush your teeth or begin your morning routine.

Bonus Benefit: By having your phone away from your bed, it provides a layer of security against wasting time using your phone before bedtime.

"I never knew a man come to greatness or eminence who lay abed late in the morning." - Johnathan Swift

Night 38

TONIGHT I'LL SLEEP AT: _____ & TOMORROW I'LL WAKE UP AT: _____

HOW HAVE I SHOWN SELF-LOVE AND CARE TO MYSELF TODAY?

_____

OPENING UP ABOUT MY DAY:

_____
_____
_____

MY MORNING RITUAL TOMORROW WILL BE: *Completed?*

1. _____ ☐
2. _____ ☐
3. _____ ☐
4. _____ ☐
5. _____ ☐

Day 39

LAST NIGHT I SLEPT AT: _____ & WOKE UP TODAY AT: _____

MY MOST IMPORTANT TASK FOR TODAY IS:

_____

WHAT IS ONE SMALL WAY I CAN IMPROVE MYSELF?

_____

Day 40: **Daily Challenge** 🔥

Challenge: Think deeply about the direct relationship between the actions you take today and your future.

Newsflash*: You are exactly a compilation of your past actions. The future version of you is exactly a compilation of the actions you take starting today.*

How do you envision yourself in the future? Successful? What actions have you taken the last month that is in direct relation to the future version of yourself you are envisioning?

One of the problems is that we believe in the possibility of a future version of ourselves that's different from who we are in this moment. We imagine that the future version of us will magically begin to take the actions towards the goals we have today, without us altering our actions today.

Our brains function off our habits. Our habits function off our actions. Our actions can only come from from the present moment.

Understand that our dream lives only exist if we change our behaviors TODAY.

☐ I completed this daily challenge.

Night 39

TONIGHT I'LL SLEEP AT: _____ & TOMORROW I'LL WAKE UP AT: _____

WHAT MEMORABLE MOMENT(S) DID I EXPERIENCE RECENTLY?

_____

OPENING UP ABOUT MY DAY:

_____

_____

_____

MY MORNING RITUAL TOMORROW WILL BE: *Completed?*

1. _____ ☐
2. _____ ☐
3. _____ ☐
4. _____ ☐
5. _____ ☐

Day 40

LAST NIGHT I SLEPT AT: _____ & WOKE UP TODAY AT: _____

MY MOST IMPORTANT TASK FOR TODAY IS:

_____

WHAT IS ONE WAY I AM NOT FULLY LIVING UP TO MY POTENTIAL?

_____

Day 41: **Pro-Tip**

<u>*Don't check your email in the mornings!*</u>

Email is notorious for being one of the most time-sucking, distracting tools out there. Here's why:

1. Email is a **reactive** tool used to respond to others. The majority of the time, it does not create any new opportunities for us.
2. Each email notification we receive throughout our day distracts us from whatever task we're working on (**this is a huge cost**).
3. When checking email on-the-go from our phones, it usually takes us much longer to go through (due to slower mobile typing speeds and a lack of navigating many webpages quickly).

The mornings are a magical time you can use for creative work. Leave mindless email until later in the day. One amazing tool you can use for this is Inbox Pause by Boomerang (no affiliation), which only pushes e-mails to your inbox at times you specify (note: as of 2018, this functionality is a paid tool).

Superhero option: turn off e-mail notifications altogether and only check it twice a day using InboxPause.

"There was never a night or problem that could defeat sunrise or hope."
- Bernard Williams

140

TONIGHT I'LL SLEEP AT: _____ & TOMORROW I'LL WAKE UP AT: _____

Night 40

WHAT IS ONE UNIQUE THING ABOUT ME THAT MAKES ME INCREDIBLY SPECIAL?

_____

OPENING UP ABOUT MY DAY:

_____

_____

_____

MY MORNING RITUAL TOMORROW WILL BE:

Completed?

(3-day challenge idea: Stretch for 2 minutes each morning.)

1. _____ ☐
2. _____ ☐
3. _____ ☐
4. _____ ☐
5. _____ ☐

Day 41

LAST NIGHT I SLEPT AT: _____ & WOKE UP TODAY AT: _____

MY MOST IMPORTANT TASK FOR TODAY IS:

_____

WHAT IS AN AREA OF WEAKNESS I HAVE IN MY LIFE THAT I WANT TO IMPROVE ON?

_____

Day 42: **Recommended Podcasts**

The Tim Ferriss Show.

Tim Ferriss' podcast has been rated the #1 podcast in the world multiple times. In his podcasts, he deconstructs the world-class performers from eclectic areas (investing, sports, business, art, etc.) to extract the tactics, tools, and routines you can use.

He's interviewed past guests such as Arnold Schwarzenegger, Jamie Foxx, Edward Norton, Tony Robbins, Maria Popova, Peter Thiel, Marc Andreessen, Amanda Palmer, Malcolm Gladwell, & more.

Towards the end of each podcast episode, Ferriss asks podcast guests what their morning routine consists of. It serves as a great example to see what some of the world's leaders are doing each morning.

Check out his podcast on ***iTunes, iHeart Radio, Stitcher***, or ***Spreaker***. To find it you can simply search "Tim Ferriss".

"The older generation thought nothing of getting up at five every morning and the younger generation doesn't think much of it either."
– John J. Welsh

Night 41

TONIGHT I'LL SLEEP AT: _____ & TOMORROW I'LL WAKE UP AT: _____

**WHAT IS A CHALLENGE - BIG OR SMALL -
I'VE SUCCESSFULLY MOVED PAST TODAY?**

_____

OPENING UP ABOUT MY DAY:

_____
_____
_____

MY MORNING RITUAL TOMORROW WILL BE:

Completed?

1. _____ ☐
2. _____ ☐
3. _____ ☐
4. _____ ☐
5. _____ ☐

Day 42

LAST NIGHT I SLEPT AT: _____ & WOKE UP TODAY AT: _____

MY MOST IMPORTANT TASK FOR TODAY IS:

_____

**WHO IS ONE PERSON WHO I CAN GIVE EXTRA
CARE AND ATTENTION TO TODAY?**

_____

Day 43: **Affirmations**

1. Find a quiet area where you can do this in private so you can be at ease. If you can't find a private space, say these in your head while pretending you're screaming them from a mountaintop.

2. Think of a time when you felt absolutely powerful - **when you felt on top of the world**. Tap into every emotion you had at that moment and get yourself into that state right now. How were you feeling then - Powerful? Unstoppable? Strong? Incredible!? Get into it now!!!!

3. Now feel your intensity grow tenfold! Say this with deep passion:

My productivity, efficiency, and energy will soar through the roof by waking up with purpose and intention.
By waking up at ____A.M., I will accomplish important and necessary tasks that lead me directly to accomplishing my life goals.
I must master this element of my life because of how much value it will add to my life and to everybody I interact with. I <u>will</u> own this.

Repeat this **one more time.**

BEING AN EARLY RISER IS BECOMING EFFORTLESS

"No matter how bad things are, you can at least be happy that you woke up this morning." – D. L Hugely

Night 42

TONIGHT I'LL SLEEP AT: _____ & TOMORROW I'LL WAKE UP AT: _____

**WHAT IS A SKILL I'VE BUILT IN MY LIFE
THAT I USED TO MY BENEFIT TODAY?**

_____

OPENING UP ABOUT MY DAY:

_____
_____
_____

MY MORNING RITUAL TOMORROW WILL BE: *Completed?*

1. _____ ☐
2. _____ ☐
3. _____ ☐
4. _____ ☐
5. _____ ☐

Day 43

LAST NIGHT I SLEPT AT: _____ & WOKE UP TODAY AT: _____

MY MOST IMPORTANT TASK FOR TODAY IS:

_____

**IF I WERE LIVING AS THE ABSOLUTE BEST VERSION OF MYSELF,
WHAT CAN I CHANGE ABOUT MY ACTIONS TODAY?**

_____

Day 44: **Pro-Tip + Affirmation** 💡 🗨

Set your intent for the morning the night before.

Imagine this: It's 11:30 P.M., you need to get up at 5 A.M. You feel the pain of only getting 5.5 hours of sleep - you've instantly communicated your dissatisfaction with your body and mind. You're now at a disadvantage —you've decided you're going to be tired and groggy due to inadequate sleep.

Try saying this out loud instead: *I will be waking up at 5:30 A.M. with an abundance of energy. I will spring out of bed ready to crush the incredible day in front of me. 5.5 hours of sleep is the perfect amount I need to be fresh and energized to have an awesome and productive day. I am grateful for the 5.5 hours of sleep I'm about to get because it is the perfect amount of sleep I need to have an amazing day!*

This 'positive thinking' approach may sound like mumbo jumbo, but genuinely do it for one night. Tailor that message however you need, but keep it positive. Send good vibes to your body, mind and heart to wake up a **winner**. If you're upset the night before regarding the amount of sleep you're about to get, you've already lost.

"Keep your dreams alive. Understand to achieve anything requires faith and belief in yourself, vision, hard work, determination, and dedication. Remember all things are possible for those who believe." - Gail Devers

TONIGHT I'LL SLEEP AT: _____ & TOMORROW I'LL WAKE UP AT: _____

Night 43

**WHAT IS ONE THING I DID TODAY THAT WILL HAVE
A CHAIN-EFFECT OF SPREADING POSITIVITY?**

_____

OPENING UP ABOUT MY DAY:

_____
_____
_____

MY MORNING RITUAL TOMORROW WILL BE: *Completed?*

1. _____ ☐
2. _____ ☐
3. _____ ☐
4. _____ ☐
5. _____ ☐

Day 44

LAST NIGHT I SLEPT AT: _____ & WOKE UP TODAY AT: _____

MY MOST IMPORTANT TASK FOR TODAY IS:

_____

WHAT CAUSES ME STRESS AND HOW COULD I BETTER RESPOND TO IT?

_____

Day 45: **Pro-Tip**

**Set your lights out (a.k.a. going to bed) time early in the day.**
**Plan your day around getting to bed at that time.**

As simple as it is, setting the time you will be in bed by is a very powerful tool. This is great for days you have a more routine schedule (usually weeknights as weekends can be a bit erratic).

Setting this time does a few things:

1. It helps you plan out the remainder of your day (e.g. how many hours you have left in the day to do what you want to do).
2. It guides you with what time you need to start preparing for bed to make sure you're ready on time.
3. It prevents you from following a string of distractions during nighttime.
4. It gives you a set time to read (reading and sleeping should be the only things that you allow yourself to do).
5. It almost guarantees your success for waking up when planned as your morning success if directly linked to what you do at night.

"Don't just drag out of bed every morning. Get alive and awaken your mind and body for the gift of a brand new day gift wrapped with sunlight and air. Not just another ordinary day, it is the day of new opportunities." – Phoebe Kites

Night 44

TONIGHT I'LL SLEEP AT: _____ & TOMORROW I'LL WAKE UP AT: _____

IF A CLOSE FRIEND SAW HOW I HANDLED MY DAY TODAY, WHAT WOULD THEY TELL ME?

_____

OPENING UP ABOUT MY DAY:

_____

_____

_____

MY MORNING RITUAL TOMORROW WILL BE: *Completed?*

1. _____ ☐
2. _____ ☐
3. _____ ☐
4. _____ ☐
5. _____ ☐

Day 45

LAST NIGHT I SLEPT AT: _____ & WOKE UP TODAY AT: _____

MY MOST IMPORTANT TASK FOR TODAY IS:

_____

IF I WERE TO MAKE NO EXCUSES FOR MY LIFE, WHAT WOULD I DO DIFFERENTLY?

_____

Day 46: **Success Story**

Tim Cook, Apple™ CEO.

The CEO of Apple™ is known for getting up and sending out company emails at 4:30 in the morning. By 5 A.M. he can be found in the gym. And he works late too, priding himself on being the first in the office and the last out. He's said to have extremely high energy levels — and he himself attributes much of his success to being an early riser and getting necessary tasks done before he goes to work.

On March 9, 2015 he tweeted at 5:31 A.M. (probably after his morning workout), "Got some extra rest for today's event. Slept in 'til 4:30." *What a beast.*

"Don't underestimate the power of thoughts and words. What you tell yourself every morning will set your mind and life on success."
- Nina Bolivares

TONIGHT I'LL SLEEP AT: _____ & TOMORROW I'LL WAKE UP AT: _____

Night 45

WHAT AM I GREAT AT THAT I DON'T GIVE MYSELF ENOUGH CREDIT FOR?

_____

OPENING UP ABOUT MY DAY:

_____

_____

_____

MY MORNING RITUAL TOMORROW WILL BE: *Completed?*

1. _____ ☐

2. _____ ☐

3. _____ ☐

4. _____ ☐

5. _____ ☐

Day 46

LAST NIGHT I SLEPT AT: _____ & WOKE UP TODAY AT: _____

MY MOST IMPORTANT TASK FOR TODAY IS:

_____

WHERE IS ONE PLACE I AM SPENDING TIME THAT DOES NOT BRING ME REAL HAPPINESS?

_____

Day 47: **Daily Challenge** 🔥

<u>*Challenge: Learn to discriminate against habitual thoughts that limit your quality and potential in life.*</u>

We ordinarily take ourselves to be our thoughts — the flow of that thought is **always** active, constantly creating the context and substance of what we're experiencing in our lives.

We are habitual animals; we are **association machines**. As we move through life, we access every association that has been created in our past related to what we're currently faced with.

The problem: When our associations are triggered through our thoughts, there isn't an active thinking process. <u>*Our past*</u> (the network of associations built based on previous experiences) answers life for us.

To create positive change, we must detach from automatic thoughts that **happen in us** when going through life. If you take a second to see the thought and recognize that you didn't actually consciously think it, a space opens up for you to think differently than your automatic self.

Realize that your initial reaction or approach can always be altered for the better. Accept the thoughts that initially come up throughout life but then **actively choose what actions you want to take.**

☐ I completed this daily challenge.

"Man is free at the moment he wishes to be." - Voltaire

Night 46

TONIGHT I'LL SLEEP AT: _____ & TOMORROW I'LL WAKE UP AT: _____

HOW HAVE I POSITIVELY IMPACTED SOMEONE'S LIFE TODAY?

_____

OPENING UP ABOUT MY DAY:

_____

_____

_____

MY MORNING RITUAL TOMORROW WILL BE: *Completed?*

1. _____ ☐

2. _____ ☐

3. _____ ☐

4. _____ ☐

5. _____ ☐

Day 47

LAST NIGHT I SLEPT AT: _____ & WOKE UP TODAY AT: _____

MY MOST IMPORTANT TASK FOR TODAY IS:

_____

WHAT IS ONE SMALL WAY I CAN IMPROVE MYSELF?

_____

Day 48: **Success Story**

<u>Richard Branson - Founder of Virgin Group</u>™

Branson wakes up at 5:45 A.M. on a daily basis, even when staying at his private island, leaving the curtains drawn so the sun gets him up. The entrepreneur even has a "Why I Wake Up Early" blog. Branson spends his mornings doing physical activity to get his energy levels up and feel his endorphins kick in with either kitesurfing, swimming or tennis.

"I have always been an early riser. Like keeping a positive outlook or keeping fit, waking up early is a habit which you must work on to maintain. Over my 50 years in business I have learned that if I rise early I can achieve so much more in a day and therefore in life.... By rising early I'm able to do some exercise and spend time with my family, which puts me in a great mind frame before getting down to business." - Richard Branson

Branson says that working out gives him at least four additional hours of productive time every day.

Consider adding exercising to your morning routine if you haven't already.

"One key to success is to have lunch at the time of day most people have breakfast." - Robert Brault

154

☁️

Night 47

TONIGHT I'LL SLEEP AT: _____ & TOMORROW I'LL WAKE UP AT: _____

🤝 **WHAT IS SOMETHING I SPENT TIME ON TODAY THAT COULD POSITIVELY IMPACT MY FUTURE?**

_____

✏️ **OPENING UP ABOUT MY DAY:**

_____
_____
_____

☀️ **MY MORNING RITUAL TOMORROW WILL BE:**   *Completed?*

(3-day challenge idea: Review 1 chapter of a beloved old book.)

1. _____ ☐
2. _____ ☐
3. _____ ☐
4. _____ ☐
5. _____ ☐

☀️

Day 48

LAST NIGHT I SLEPT AT: _____ & WOKE UP TODAY AT: _____

🐸 **MY MOST IMPORTANT TASK FOR TODAY IS:**

_____

🕐 **WHAT IS ONE TIME I WANT TO BE MORE PRESENT AND LESS DISTRACTED DURING MY DAY?**

_____

155

Day 49: **YouTube Alert!**

FitLife.Tv with Drew Canole.

Drew's story is a very inspiring one. He went from being ~20% body fat to less than 7%! He lives a happy, healthy lifestyle and is great at providing actionable guidance for you to follow.

Drew has done a lot of research on nutrition and is a huge proponent of using vegetable juicing to cut fat and increase the amount of micronutrients your body is getting.

Drew's channel focuses not only on building a healthy morning routine, but also is a great starting point for anybody looking to take their nutrition to the next level, to cut fat, pack on muscle, and overall increase their body's health & happiness every day!

Recommended video to search on YouTube: 7 Step Morning Ritual with Drew Canole

Subscribe here: **www.youtube.com/user/fitlifetv**

"In the morning a man walks with his whole body; in the evening, just with his legs." - Ralph Waldo Emerson

Night 48

TONIGHT I'LL SLEEP AT: _____ & TOMORROW I'LL WAKE UP AT: _____

WHAT IS ONE EMOTIONAL RESPONSE I HAD TODAY THAT I AM PROUD OF?

_____

OPENING UP ABOUT MY DAY:

_____

_____

_____

MY MORNING RITUAL TOMORROW WILL BE: *Completed?*

1. _____ ☐
2. _____ ☐
3. _____ ☐
4. _____ ☐
5. _____ ☐

Day 49

LAST NIGHT I SLEPT AT: _____ & WOKE UP TODAY AT: _____

MY MOST IMPORTANT TASK FOR TODAY IS:

_____

WHEN WAS THE LAST TIME I DID NOT STICK TO MY WORD? HOW CAN I AVOID DOING SO AGAIN?

_____

Day 50: **Pro-Tip**

Wait until you finish your morning ritual before using your phone.

Bathe, get dressed and groom before you switch on your smart phone (or take it out of airplane mode). You'll be fully ready to tackle the day ahead versus sitting around in your pajamas and bathrobe fiddling with your phone. Not only does it help you avoid wasting the extremely valuable morning hours, but you'll notice just how correlated stress is with your phone. This is because your phone is really your outlet to the world. Your outlet to work, to social media, and there's a lot of anxiety that comes with those outlets.

Try as long as possible to avoid messing around with your phone until you absolutely need to use it when your day has started. It'll do you wonders!

Going in airplane mode when you go to sleep and leaving your phone off until you complete your morning ritual will set you up for success here.

"Every morning in Africa, a Gazelle wakes up. It knows it must run faster than the fastest lion or it will be killed. Every morning a Lion wakes up. It knows it must outrun the slowest Gazelle or it will starve to death. It doesn't matter whether you are a Lion or a Gazelle... when the sun comes up, you'd better be running." - Anonymous

Night 49

TONIGHT I'LL SLEEP AT: _____ & TOMORROW I'LL WAKE UP AT: _____

HOW HAS MY OUTLOOK ON LIFE IMPROVED MY DAY?

_____

OPENING UP ABOUT MY DAY:

_____

_____

_____

MY MORNING RITUAL TOMORROW WILL BE: *Completed?*

1. _____ ☐
2. _____ ☐
3. _____ ☐
4. _____ ☐
5. _____ ☐

Day 50

LAST NIGHT I SLEPT AT: _____ & WOKE UP TODAY AT: _____

MY MOST IMPORTANT TASK FOR TODAY IS:

_____

WHAT IS ONE AREA I CAN APPROACH WITH MORE ENTHUSIASM AND ENERGY TODAY?

_____

Day 51: **Favorite Resources** ¶¶

Dance, party, and jumpstart your day at 6 A.M. at Daybreaker!

Does the sound of a 6 A.M. morning dance party spark any excitement in you?? Well that's what a Daybreaker is— one of the absolute BEST ways to start off your morning.

Daybreaker is truly a one-of-a-kind event. The community there is AMAZING. It's full of love, acceptance, happiness, and dancing. Also, instead of alcohol, they serve healthy snacks and coffee.

They're a relatively new company but are expanding quickly. If they're not in your city, you can petition them to move there too.

Check Daybreaker out here: **www.Daybreaker.com**

Fun fact: After Mikey (one of the coauthors of this journal) missed a Daybreaker event by not being able to wake up early, he set out to change his morning habits. This journal would likely not be in existence if it weren't for Daybreaker!

"Front-loading my day (getting a whole bunch done in the morning) is my productivity secret." – Celeste Headlee

TONIGHT I'LL SLEEP AT: _____ & TOMORROW I'LL WAKE UP AT: _____

Night 50

HOW HAVE I SET MY FUTURE SELF UP FOR SUCCESS TODAY?

_____

OPENING UP ABOUT MY DAY:

_____

_____

_____

MY MORNING RITUAL TOMORROW WILL BE: _Completed?_

1. _____ ☐

2. _____ ☐

3. _____ ☐

4. _____ ☐

5. _____ ☐

Day 51

LAST NIGHT I SLEPT AT: _____ & WOKE UP TODAY AT: _____

MY MOST IMPORTANT TASK FOR TODAY IS:

_____

WHO IS SOMEONE THAT WILL HAVE A POSITIVE EFFECT IN MY LIFE THAT I SHOULD SPEND MORE TIME WITH?

_____

Day 52: **Affirmations**

1. Find a quiet area where you can do this in private so you can be at ease. If you can't find a private space, say these in your head while pretending you're screaming them from a mountaintop.

2. Think of a time when you felt absolutely powerful - **when you felt on top of the world**. Tap into every emotion you had at that moment and get yourself into that state right now. How were you feeling then - Powerful? Unstoppable? Strong? Incredible!? Get into it now!!!!

3. Now feel your intensity grow tenfold! Say this with deep passion:

I am noticing that waking up when I choose is requiring less and less effort. I am turning into someone who immediately wakes up as soon as my alarm goes off. I will take full advantage of every day by waking up when is best for ME.

I must minimize my distractions at night, disconnect from time-sucking applications and unfulfilling entertainment, and I will move head-first to achieving incredible clarity and success in my life!

Repeat this **one more time.**

I WILL ACCOMPLISH IMPORTANT AND NECESSARY TASKS TODAY BECAUSE I AM FOCUSED AND ENERGIZED FROM MY MORNING RITUAL

"The way I define happiness is being the creator of your experience, choosing to take pleasure in what you have, right now, regardless of the circumstances, while being the best you that you can be." - Leo Babauta

Night 51

TONIGHT I'LL SLEEP AT: _____ & TOMORROW I'LL WAKE UP AT: _____

HOW HAVE I SHOWN SELF-LOVE AND CARE TO MYSELF TODAY?

_____

OPENING UP ABOUT MY DAY:

_____
_____
_____

MY MORNING RITUAL TOMORROW WILL BE: *Completed?*

1. _____ ☐
2. _____ ☐
3. _____ ☐
4. _____ ☐
5. _____ ☐

Day 52

LAST NIGHT I SLEPT AT: _____ & WOKE UP TODAY AT: _____

MY MOST IMPORTANT TASK FOR TODAY IS:

_____

WHAT IS ONE SMALL WAY I CAN IMPROVE MYSELF?

_____

Day 53: **Daily Challenge** 🔥

Challenge: Regardless of your mood or energy levels in the mornings, let your actions set the tone for your day.

Although some morning people wake up full of energy and ready to start their day every day... the majority wake up *just as tired* as everybody else. But the ones who really conquer their mornings are the ones who take massive action to fill their bodies up with energy throughout that phase of being tired. These are the people who literally create energy within their bodies by forcing themselves to move quickly and powerfully.

Your body's energy levels are much harder to change through mental battles (e.g. trying to motivate yourself to get out of bed) versus **taking action** (e.g. forcing yourself to jump out of bed and MOVE!)

In summary:
- Your mindset changes from your actions.
- Your actions are what you always have control over (while you can't control the thoughts that come through your head).
- So take the right actions to succeed regardless of your emotional state... your emotions will be set by the actions you take.

> ☐ I completed this daily challenge.

NO MATTER HOW TIRED I AM, I WILL KEEP MOVING

"Life is too short," she panicked, "I want more." He nodded slowly, "Wake up earlier."- Dr. SunWolf

TONIGHT I'LL SLEEP AT: _____ & TOMORROW I'LL WAKE UP AT: _____

Night 52

WHAT MEMORABLE MOMENT(S) DID I EXPERIENCE RECENTLY?

_____

OPENING UP ABOUT MY DAY:

_____
_____
_____

MY MORNING RITUAL TOMORROW WILL BE: _Completed?_

1. _____   ☐
2. _____   ☐
3. _____   ☐
4. _____   ☐
5. _____   ☐

Day 53

LAST NIGHT I SLEPT AT: _____ & WOKE UP TODAY AT: _____

MY MOST IMPORTANT TASK FOR TODAY IS:

_____

WHAT IS ONE WAY I AM NOT FULLY LIVING UP TO MY POTENTIAL?

_____

Day 54: **Pro-Tip**

Jumpstart your day by taking a cold shower.

Cold showers are one of the greatest tests of discipline out there. And once you conquer them, you feel **_unstoppable_**.

Cold showers accomplish the following:
1. Floods your body with health benefits (amazing for your cardiovascular system).
2. Physically shocks your body to wake up and feel full of energy. This is incredibly useful for turbocharging your mornings.
3. Makes you feel like a mental warrior who can conquer anything.
4. Trains your discipline which carries into building other habits.

A great approach is to ease into cold showers. Start hot and each shower make it about 2-5% colder. As time goes on it's very common to genuinely prefer cold showers to hot ones, or at least a mix of both. Ending with cold for 30 seconds is best.

Double Pro-Tip: Getting a waterproof shower speaker makes this process a lot more enjoyable too (dancing through the cold is VERY effective). They're fairly inexpensive on Amazon.

"Don't underestimate the power of thoughts and words. What you tell yourself every morning will set your mind and life on that path. Talk success, victory, happiness and blessings over your destiny."
– Nina Bolivares

Night 53

TONIGHT I'LL SLEEP AT: _____ & TOMORROW I'LL WAKE UP AT: _____

WHAT IS ONE UNIQUE THING ABOUT ME THAT MAKES ME INCREDIBLY SPECIAL?

_____

OPENING UP ABOUT MY DAY:

_____
_____
_____

MY MORNING RITUAL TOMORROW WILL BE: _Completed?_

(3-day challenge idea: Walk 2 blocks while listening to a podcast.)

1. _____ ☐
2. _____ ☐
3. _____ ☐
4. _____ ☐
5. _____ ☐

Day 54

LAST NIGHT I SLEPT AT: _____ & WOKE UP TODAY AT: _____

MY MOST IMPORTANT TASK FOR TODAY IS:

_____

WHAT IS AN AREA OF WEAKNESS I HAVE IN MY LIFE THAT I WANT TO IMPROVE ON?

_____

Day 55: **User Success Story**

Andrew Taylor, Morning Sidekick Journal User.

Andrew's biggest challenge when it came to changing his morning routine:
"The biggest challenge for me is addressing the competing priorities I have in my work and personal life, plus the fact that both my work and family schedule can be a bit unpredictable. The solution for me is to have a collection of multiple routines that I use for different days of the week, while still getting up at the same time every day. Sometimes this is hard to do when traveling for work, but when I can't do the whole morning routine, I try to at least do a portion of it, regardless of where I am."

Andrew challenges other Morning Sidekick Journal users to:
"Think of just one goal that really matters to you that requires intention and concentration. Next, think of a way to break that goal into small pieces and work on it during the mornings. You will be amazed at what is possible."

One game-changing mindset Andrew uses consistently:
"I have found that when I can reframe some of the toughest moments I have experienced as opportunities to learn, they become amazing growth opportunities. In fact, some of the hardest things I have experienced in my career and personal life have produced the most lasting change and growth for me."

"Nothing is as strong as gentleness, and nothing is as gentle as real strength." - Saint Francis de Sales

TONIGHT I'LL SLEEP AT: _____ & TOMORROW I'LL WAKE UP AT: _____

Night 54

**WHAT IS A CHALLENGE - BIG OR SMALL -
I'VE SUCCESSFULLY MOVED PAST TODAY?**

_____

OPENING UP ABOUT MY DAY:

_____

_____

_____

MY MORNING RITUAL TOMORROW WILL BE: _Completed?_

1. _____ ☐

2. _____ ☐

3. _____ ☐

4. _____ ☐

5. _____ ☐

Day 55

LAST NIGHT I SLEPT AT: _____ & WOKE UP TODAY AT: _____

MY MOST IMPORTANT TASK FOR TODAY IS:

_____

**WHO IS ONE PERSON WHO I CAN GIVE EXTRA
CARE AND ATTENTION TO TODAY?**

_____

169

Day 56: **Daily Challenge** 🔥

Challenge: Write down your morning routine from least difficult to most difficult activities & do them in that order.

A very good practice is to think about all of the things that absolutely must get done in a day and work them into chains. Unless the order actually matters, the easiest habits should be loaded up front, and the most difficult ones should be left for last.

This ensures that you maximize the benefit of momentum as you move through your chain. Every small victory you win by moving through the chain gives you the power to finish it off strongly. The sequence of easiest activities to most difficult will provide you with a sense of satisfaction and confidence that you can build on.

It's through this process that habits give you freedom – chains take care of the necessities of life and leave you with time and willpower to make forward progress.

☐ I completed this daily challenge.

"Giving myself time, care, and attention in the morning has been crucial to significantly reducing my stress levels and consistently increasing my capacity to perform, have clarity, and take action."
– Aiste Gazdar

Night 55

TONIGHT I'LL SLEEP AT: _____ & TOMORROW I'LL WAKE UP AT: _____

WHAT IS A SKILL I'VE BUILT IN MY LIFE THAT I USED TO MY BENEFIT TODAY?

_____

OPENING UP ABOUT MY DAY:

_____

_____

_____

MY MORNING RITUAL TOMORROW WILL BE:

Completed?

1. _____ ☐
2. _____ ☐
3. _____ ☐
4. _____ ☐
5. _____ ☐

Day 56

LAST NIGHT I SLEPT AT: _____ & WOKE UP TODAY AT: _____

MY MOST IMPORTANT TASK FOR TODAY IS:

_____

IF I WERE LIVING AS THE ABSOLUTE BEST VERSION OF MYSELF, WHAT CAN I CHANGE ABOUT MY ACTIONS TODAY?

_____

171

Day 57: **Pro-Tip**

Eat healthy - smaller decisions have chain effects on your day.

Decisions like what kind of food you eat, whether you start a difficult task or procrastinate, or whether you clarify an internal stress or let it go unnoticed, all have compounding effects way into your life's future.

Very commonly, yet unknowingly, these smaller decisions lead to a chain of effects that will negatively effect us. A heavy meal will lead to feeling slow and unproductive. This will lead to poor leadership and decision making. This will cause problems that need precious time to get fixed and important work to go unfinished. Chances are this will lead to stress, guilt, which will thus lead to making poor decisions once again that will continue the cycle.

Keep this chain of effects in mind when making smaller decisions throughout your day - remember the implications go way farther than just now. A poor decision now is practically equivalent to shooting your future self in the foot… just hours ahead.

"I have always been delighted at the prospect of a new day, a fresh try, one more start, with perhaps a bit of magic waiting somewhere behind the morning." - B. Priestley

Night 56

TONIGHT I'LL SLEEP AT: _____ & TOMORROW I'LL WAKE UP AT: _____

WHAT IS ONE THING I DID TODAY THAT WILL HAVE A CHAIN-EFFECT OF SPREADING POSITIVITY?

_____

OPENING UP ABOUT MY DAY:

_____
_____
_____

MY MORNING RITUAL TOMORROW WILL BE: *Completed?*

1. _____ ☐
2. _____ ☐
3. _____ ☐
4. _____ ☐
5. _____ ☐

Day 57

LAST NIGHT I SLEPT AT: _____ & WOKE UP TODAY AT: _____

MY MOST IMPORTANT TASK FOR TODAY IS:

_____

WHAT CAUSES ME STRESS AND HOW COULD I BETTER RESPOND TO IT?

_____

Day 58: YouTube Alert! ▶

Robin Sharma.

Robin Sharma is a well-known best-selling author and speaker who has dedicated his life to helping people transform their lives in personal and professional settings. He's authored 15 global best-sellers and he's an absolute expert on leadership. He has a lot of insight to give to the world. Check out the link below about waking up early and see what other pieces of treasure you can find in his videos!

Some topics he covers: Waking up early, meditation, increasing willpower, beating procrastination, genuinely living happily every day.

Search this video on YouTube: **Robin Sharma on "How to Wake Up Early"**
Subscribe for free here: **www.youtube.com/user/sharmaleadership**

"The secret of your future is hidden in your daily routine."
- Mike Murdock

Night 57

TONIGHT I'LL SLEEP AT: _____ & TOMORROW I'LL WAKE UP AT: _____

IF A CLOSE FRIEND SAW HOW I HANDLED MY DAY TODAY, WHAT WOULD THEY TELL ME?

_____

OPENING UP ABOUT MY DAY:

_____

_____

_____

MY MORNING RITUAL TOMORROW WILL BE: *Completed?*

1. _____   ☐
2. _____   ☐
3. _____   ☐
4. _____   ☐
5. _____   ☐

Day 58

LAST NIGHT I SLEPT AT: _____ & WOKE UP TODAY AT: _____

MY MOST IMPORTANT TASK FOR TODAY IS:

_____

IF I WERE TO MAKE NO EXCUSES FOR MY LIFE, WHAT WOULD I DO DIFFERENTLY?

_____

175

Day 59: **Success Story**

Oprah Winfrey, founder of OWN; media icon.

Oprah, the queen herself, is a big proponent of using mornings to start your day off with incredible momentum.

She wakes up between 6:02am and 6:20am without an alarm (she sets the number in her head each night before! Wow). She makes a cappuccino then works out with the elliptical machine and treadmill.

What sticks out the most is she makes sure to meditate each morning. **Even when she's in a rush, she prioritizes** it and does at least 10 minutes (though usually she aims for 20). She even has a specific meditation room in her house to help with this.

If she's not tapping into things she's grateful for in the morning, she has loads of gratitude journals she uses at night.

Have you considered how you could use meditation or gratitude (or both) in your morning routine?

"Be thankful for what you have; you'll end up having more. If you concentrate on what you don't have, you will never, ever have enough."- Oprah Winfrey

TONIGHT I'LL SLEEP AT: _____ & TOMORROW I'LL WAKE UP AT: _____

Night 58

WHAT AM I GREAT AT THAT I DON'T GIVE MYSELF ENOUGH CREDIT FOR?

_____

OPENING UP ABOUT MY DAY:

_____

_____

_____

MY MORNING RITUAL TOMORROW WILL BE: *Completed?*

(3-day
challenge
idea: Watch 1
TED talk
each
morning.)

1. _____ ☐
2. _____ ☐
3. _____ ☐
4. _____ ☐
5. _____ ☐

Day 59

LAST NIGHT I SLEPT AT: _____ & WOKE UP TODAY AT: _____

MY MOST IMPORTANT TASK FOR TODAY IS:

_____

WHERE IS ONE PLACE I AM SPENDING TIME THAT DOES NOT BRING ME REAL HAPPINESS?

_____

Day 60: **Pro-Tip**

<u>*Order a new Sidekick Journal to continue mastering your habits.*</u>

Heads up: you're on the final pages of this journal!

If you're one of the few who's made it this far, don't lose momentum now. You're entering the time where you can consistently reap the benefits of building up habits.

If you'd like to continue holding yourself accountable to this habit, we created followup volumes of the *Morning Sidekick Journal*. The full *Morning Sidekick Journal* series spans over the course of a year!

And if you're hungry for more, you can continue tracking your mornings while also starting to build a new habit! As of January 2019, these are the other habit journals we offer:

- *The Nutrition & Weight Management Sidekick Journal*
- *The Meditation Sidekick Journal*
- *The Badass Body Goals Fitness Journal*
- *The Weightlifting Gym Buddy*
- *The Greatest Gift* (an all-in-one gratitude scrapbooking kit)

See more at: **habitnest.com**
Note: You can get a sneak peek of these all after day 66 of this journal.

"With the new day comes new strength and new thoughts."
– Eleanor Roosevelt

Night 59

TONIGHT I'LL SLEEP AT: _____ & TOMORROW I'LL WAKE UP AT: _____

HOW HAVE I POSITIVELY IMPACTED SOMEONE'S LIFE TODAY?

_____

OPENING UP ABOUT MY DAY:

_____

_____

_____

MY MORNING RITUAL TOMORROW WILL BE: *Completed?*

1. _____ ☐

2. _____ ☐

3. _____ ☐

4. _____ ☐

5. _____ ☐

Day 60

LAST NIGHT I SLEPT AT: _____ & WOKE UP TODAY AT: _____

MY MOST IMPORTANT TASK FOR TODAY IS:

_____

WHAT IS ONE SMALL WAY I CAN IMPROVE MYSELF?

_____

Day 61: **Affirmations**

1. Find a quiet area where you can do this in private so you can be at ease. If you can't find a private space, say these in your head while pretending you're screaming them from a mountaintop.

2. Think of a time when you felt absolutely powerful - **when you felt on top of the world.** Tap into every emotion you had at that moment and get yourself into that state right now. How were you feeling then - Powerful? Unstoppable? Strong? Incredible!? Get into it now!!!!

3. Now feel your intensity grow tenfold! Say this with deep passion:

Consistently doing my morning routine sparks newfound energy levels and work ethic inside me every day. It skyrockets me on my path to becoming the best version of myself.

By becoming the best version of myself, I am able to spread more love to my friends, family, and everybody around me. I am the leading force behind an ever-growing beacon of positivity in the world!

Repeat this **one more time.**

"Life begins at the end of your comfort zone." – Neale Donald Walsh

Night 60

TONIGHT I'LL SLEEP AT: _____ & TOMORROW I'LL WAKE UP AT: _____

WHAT IS SOMETHING I SPENT TIME ON TODAY THAT COULD POSITIVELY IMPACT MY FUTURE?

_____

OPENING UP ABOUT MY DAY:

_____

_____

_____

MY MORNING RITUAL TOMORROW WILL BE: *Completed?*

1. _____ ☐
2. _____ ☐
3. _____ ☐
4. _____ ☐
5. _____ ☐

Day 61

LAST NIGHT I SLEPT AT: _____ & WOKE UP TODAY AT: _____

MY MOST IMPORTANT TASK FOR TODAY IS:

_____

WHAT IS ONE TIME I WANT TO BE MORE PRESENT AND LESS DISTRACTED DURING MY DAY?

_____

Day 62: **Pro-Tip**

**Smile at yourself in the mirror for 30 seconds.**

This is a can't-miss way to boost your self esteem. Once you get into the habit you'll wonder how you ever got along without it.

Make sure you're smiling; it doesn't have to be a big goofy grin, just the hint of a smile works. This works on a number of different levels, but at the core is the ability it gives you to establish a positive, love-filled relationship with yourself before the day starts.

It's not easy to try this exercise even once and not feel a little bit crazy.

That being said, this one is incredibly effective. The exercise of literally smiling in front of a mirror has been linked to squandering depression and melting away the stresses that secretly build up in us.

What you're doing here is basically checking in with your mind and body on the deepest level. By giving yourself a deep physiological message that you are happy, you force your body to adapt. And daily happiness in 30 seconds can go a long ways.

"Every morning brings new potential, but if you tend to dwell on the misfortunes of the day before, you tend to overlook tremendous opportunities." - Harvey Mackay

Night 61

TONIGHT I'LL SLEEP AT: _____ & TOMORROW I'LL WAKE UP AT: _____

WHAT IS ONE EMOTIONAL RESPONSE I HAD TODAY THAT I AM PROUD OF?

_____

OPENING UP ABOUT MY DAY:

_____

_____

_____

MY MORNING RITUAL TOMORROW WILL BE: *Completed?*

1. _____ ☐

2. _____ ☐

3. _____ ☐

4. _____ ☐

5. _____ ☐

Day 62

LAST NIGHT I SLEPT AT: _____ & WOKE UP TODAY AT: _____

MY MOST IMPORTANT TASK FOR TODAY IS:

_____

WHEN WAS THE LAST TIME I DID NOT STICK TO MY WORD? HOW CAN I AVOID DOING SO AGAIN?

_____

Day 63: **Affirmations**

1. Find a quiet area where you can do this in private so you can be at ease. If you can't find a private space, say these in your head while pretending you're screaming them from a mountaintop.

2. Think of a time when you felt absolutely powerful - **when you felt on top of the world**. Tap into every emotion you had at that moment and get yourself into that state right now. How were you feeling then - Powerful? Unstoppable? Strong? Incredible!? Get into it now!!!!

3. Now feel your intensity grow tenfold! Say this with deep passion:

---

*Day after day, I am realizing that my potential in life is **absolutely limitless**. I am an unstoppable force for good.*

I am going to destroy every obstacle and challenge that comes in my path because I know that nothing is bigger than me.

By improving myself every day, day after day after day, I am creating a snowball effect that will propel me through life to incredible success.

Repeat this **one more time.**

TONIGHT I'LL SLEEP AT: _____ & TOMORROW I'LL WAKE UP AT: _____

Night 62

HOW HAS MY OUTLOOK ON LIFE IMPROVED MY DAY?

_____

OPENING UP ABOUT MY DAY:

_____

_____

_____

MY MORNING RITUAL TOMORROW WILL BE: _Completed?_

1. _____ ☐
2. _____ ☐
3. _____ ☐
4. _____ ☐
5. _____ ☐

Day 63

LAST NIGHT I SLEPT AT: _____ & WOKE UP TODAY AT: _____

MY MOST IMPORTANT TASK FOR TODAY IS:

_____

WHAT IS ONE AREA I CAN APPROACH WITH MORE ENTHUSIASM AND ENERGY TODAY?

_____

Day 64: **Pro-Tip**

<u>The next time you feel 'out of it,' take physical action (not mental) to shift your body's state.</u>

Preparing for your off days and days of struggle is absolutely critical. It's what many of the Pro-Tips in this book cover. Shifting your off days to work in your favor is what's most challenging, yet the most rewarding.

Let's be real - having an off day is inevitable and you will absolutely hit another point where you feel like total crap. Trying to mentally battle yourself to 'feel better' won't do you any good in this state.

What IS incredibly effective is taking a **physical action** to shock your body physiologically. The next time you feel out of it, force yourself to take a physical action to shift your body's state (by boosting oxygen, adrenaline, and/or endorphins). Some specific actions you can take the next time you feel out of it are:

1.   Take 5 long inhales deep into your stomach.
2.   Work out or move around (even for 30 seconds).
3.   Take a cold shower (this is for the truly crazy ones out there).

"Early rising not only gives us more life in the same number of years, but adds, likewise, to their number; and not only enables us to enjoy more of existence in the same time, but increases also the measure."
- Caleb C. Colton

Night 63

TONIGHT I'LL SLEEP AT: _____ & TOMORROW I'LL WAKE UP AT: _____

HOW HAVE I SET MY FUTURE SELF UP FOR SUCCESS TODAY?

_____

OPENING UP ABOUT MY DAY:

_____

_____

_____

MY MORNING RITUAL TOMORROW WILL BE: *Completed?*

1. _____ ☐
2. _____ ☐
3. _____ ☐
4. _____ ☐
5. _____ ☐

Day 64

LAST NIGHT I SLEPT AT: _____ & WOKE UP TODAY AT: _____

MY MOST IMPORTANT TASK FOR TODAY IS:

_____

WHO IS SOMEONE THAT WILL HAVE A POSITIVE EFFECT IN MY LIFE THAT I SHOULD SPEND MORE TIME WITH?

_____

Day 65: **Success Story**

<u>*Scott Adams, creator of Dilbert*™</u>

Business Insider reported that Adams designs his morning routine to maximize his creativity. Adams was quoted saying, "My value is based on my best ideas in any given day, not the number of hours I work."

Adams has a protein bar and coffee every morning. "I give myself this 'treat' knowing I can be trained like any other animal. And I want to train myself to enjoy waking up and being productive (it totally works)."

Have you considered implementing any morning routines to stimulate creativity for the rest of the day? One that comes to mind is brainstorming out 10 ideas (about anything!) as recommended by author James Altucher.

"My morning routine definitely sets the tone for the rest of my day. If I'm rushed and stressed in the morning, that will carry through my work day."
– Tessa Miller

DATE _____

Night 64

TONIGHT I'LL SLEEP AT: _____ & TOMORROW I'LL WAKE UP AT: _____

HOW HAVE I SHOWN SELF-LOVE AND CARE TO MYSELF TODAY?

_____

OPENING UP ABOUT MY DAY:

_____
_____
_____

MY MORNING RITUAL TOMORROW WILL BE: *Completed?*

1. _____ ☐
2. _____ ☐
3. _____ ☐
4. _____ ☐
5. _____ ☐

Day 65

LAST NIGHT I SLEPT AT: _____ & WOKE UP TODAY AT: _____

MY MOST IMPORTANT TASK FOR TODAY IS:

_____

WHAT IS ONE WAY I AM NOT FULLY LIVING UP TO MY POTENTIAL?

_____

189

Day 66: **Congratulations!!!** 🥂

You've made it to the end of the journal. **You now OWN your mornings,** one of the most difficult habits to master in your life.

For you to have gotten this far means you've earned a very serious congratulations. You need to celebrate because your willpower and confidence should be soaring through the roof. You've gained lessons about yourself not many dare to approach. You've struggled with your own mind, body and heart and gained some serious control over them. You fully understand that you have the power in you to accomplish ANY goal you put your mind to.

This is a skill you've built inside you that you can turn on whenever you need it at any future point in your lifetime. **That's so awesome.**

You are a WARRIOR and we (Amir, Ari, & Mikey) hope you continue to build on your habit success and personal development for the rest of your life.

Note: The first question we get from users who finish the journal is "What should I do now?" For that reason we created followup journal volumes to the Morning Sidekick Journal!

If you think it'd be useful for you to continue growing with this practice, you can find out more here: habitnest.com/morningseries

Night 65

TONIGHT I'LL SLEEP AT: _____ & TOMORROW I'LL WAKE UP AT: _____

HOW HAS MY OUTLOOK ON LIFE IMPROVED MY DAY?

_____

OPENING UP ABOUT MY DAY:

_____

_____

_____

MY MORNING RITUAL TOMORROW WILL BE: *Completed?*

1. _____ ☐

2. _____ ☐

3. _____ ☐

4. _____ ☐

5. _____ ☐

Day 66

LAST NIGHT I SLEPT AT: _____ & WOKE UP TODAY AT: _____

MY MOST IMPORTANT TASK FOR TODAY IS:

_____

WHAT IS ONE SMALL WAY I CAN IMPROVE MYSELF?

_____

PHASE ~~3.~~

COMPLETED.

Phase 3 Recap: Days 22-66+

1. Think about what your life looked like before you began this habit — what are you doing differently now? How do you feel?

_____

_____

_____

_____

2. What unforeseen effects has your life gained from all this?

_____

_____

_____

_____

3. When you are struggling with this habit in the future, what are the key factors you should remember to do again?

_____

_____

_____

4. What daily tracking and accountability can you have going forward to maintain the momentum you've built here?

_____

_____

- Fin -

So... What Now?

Although you should feel very accomplished for getting through this entire journal… know that you built this habit to *continually improve your life. Don't stop now. This is only the beginning.*

One huge factor to this is tracking your progress. Once you stop tracking, it makes it exponentially easier for you to skip having a productive morning (due to the lack of accountability with yourself).

Remember: **Every single day in your life where you start your morning with focus, intent, and energy will automatically be a better day of your life.**

You only stand to gain from continuing this habit.

Continuing the Habit

As of Summer 2019, we've launched new followup journals to the **Morning Sidekick Journal:**

- *The Morning Sidekick Journal - Volume I*
- *The Morning Sidekick Journal - Volume II*
- *The Morning Sidekick Journal - Volume III*
- *The Morning Mastery Journal - Volume ∞*

Each new volume includes:

- Three **themed 21-day Sprints** to help you explore new areas of your life. In Volume II, these are **Gratitude, Self-Care, and Building Confidence.**
- Each Sprint contains **brand new tracking questions** that are specific to that phase!
- Each volume has 63 days of **brand new daily content** to keep things fresh!

If you feel continuing this process will add value to your life, you can get yours here!

habitnest.com/morningseries

<u>**Volume II**</u>

Sample Content Day: **Pro-Tip**

<u>*The importance of your last thoughts of the day.*</u>

Hal Elrod, author of *The Miracle Morning*, says that the last thought you have before going to bed is the first one you'll have when waking up.

If you spend a minute or two before going to bed thinking about how you want to begin the day, visualizing your morning routine, and thinking about the type of energy levels you want to have in the morning, it can play a crucial role in how you actually feel when you wake up.

It's sort of like choosing what you're going to experience when you wake up by thinking about it and telling yourself that's how it's going to be. Our minds are incredibly powerful, and what we believe about what we're experiencing dictates much of the experience.

This visualization can give you the right guidance to wake up on time and jump out of bed, ready to start your day with passion (instead of letting your tired, unmotivated brain take over)!

"Set a goal that makes you want to jump out of bed in the morning."
- Brian Tracy

Sample Tracking Day

DATE _____

Night 00

TONIGHT I'LL SLEEP AT: _____ & TOMORROW I'LL WAKE UP AT: _____

NEW

(Here is a sample of a question from the 'Gratitude' sprint!)

WHAT AM I MOST GRATEFUL FOR TODAY?

_____

_____

_____

WHAT IS A CHALLENGE - BIG OR SMALL - I'VE SUCCESSFULLY MOVED PAST TODAY?

_____

MY MORNING RITUAL TOMORROW WILL BE: *Completed?*

1. _____ ☐
2. _____ ☐
3. _____ ☐
4. _____ ☐
5. _____ ☐

Day 01

LAST NIGHT I SLEPT AT: _____ & WOKE UP TODAY AT: _____

MY MOST IMPORTANT TASK FOR TODAY IS:

_____

WHAT IS AN AREA OF WEAKNESS I HAVE IN MY LIFE THAT I WANT TO IMPROVE ON?

_____

8.5

Meet the Habit Nest Team

Amir Atighehchi graduated from USC's Marshall School of Business in 2013. He got his first taste of entrepreneurship during college with Mikey when they co-founded a bicycle lock company called *Nutlock*. It wasn't until after college when he opened his eyes to the world of personal development and healthy habits. Amir is fascinated by creative challenges and entrepreneurship.

Mikey Ahdoot transformed his life from a 200+ pound video game addict to someone who was completing 17 daily habits consistently at one point. From ice cold showers to brainstorming 10 ideas a day (shoutout to James Altucher) to celebrating life every single day, he is first-hand becoming a habit routine machine that sets himself up for success daily. He is a graduate of USC's Marshall School of Business and a proud Trojan.

Ari Banayan graduated from the University of Southern California Gould School of Law in 2016. Through his own life experience, he understands how important it is to take care of ourselves mentally, physically and emotionally to operate at maximum capacity. He uses waking up early, reading, meditation, exercise, and a healthy diet to create a solid foundation for his everyday life.

Read all of our full stories here:

habitnest.com/about-us

Shop Habit Nest Products

Meditation Sidekick
Journal

The *Meditation Sidekick Journal* is built to help two types of people:

1. To help **newcomers or past strugglers** to easily own the practice of meditation.

2. To help **constant meditators** push their practice to another level.

Layout of the Journal

1. **Building the foundation** - get a quick insight into the *science behind meditation* and clarity of what you're likely to experience during it.

2. **Accountability** - track your practice daily to see your progress and hold yourself accountable in staying consistent.

3. **Learn in bite-sized chunks** - get daily exposure to different types of meditations (e.g. transcendental, gratitude, physical body, etc.) and see which ones impact your life the most.

One thing we love: The journal is not just designed to help you meditate effectively, but more importantly, to **help you reach the end goal of consistently living mindfully every day.**

Get yours at **habitnest.com/meditation**

Sample Journal Page

 TODAY I WILL MEDITATE AT:

7:30 a.m. ✓

 FOR AT LEAST:

5 minutes ✓

ONE UPCOMING MENTAL OR EMOTIONAL HURDLE TO BE MINDFUL OF:

My presentation for my boss at work - own it!

 BENEFITS I FELT TODAY (CIRCLE):

 Feel Happier

 More Creative

 Increased Willpower

 Improved Focus

 More Energized

 Reduced Stress

WHAT DOES MY INTERNAL DIALOGUE CONSIST OF?

I realize that I think about my appearance A LOT...
and I immediately assume people judge me for it.

ONE SMALL WAY I CAN IMPROVE MY INTERNAL DIALOGUE:

I could be more understanding when I'm feeling self-conscious and willingly accept myself for how I look.

OPENING UP ABOUT MY DAY:

Today was a rollercoaster. I realize that when I'm working with others, I prefer not to rely on them to get things done. It's something I want to work on improving because I make myself feel anxious when it happens.

203

Nutrition Sidekick
Journal

The Nutrition Sidekick Journal has a similar layout to *The Morning Sidekick Journal*. It's designed to be flexible and adaptable to whatever food goals you may have. It can be used to successfully implement:

- Calorie counting
- Weight management and/or muscle building
- General healthy eating
- Paleo / vegan / IIFYM / ketosis / other custom diets

The journal serves as your personal trainer for losing weight and **regaining control over your eating habits** quickly and effectively.

It allows you to **perfectly track** all that you need for YOUR body's optimum nutrition. These include:

- Daily caloric intake goal
- Water drinking goal
- Exercise goal
- Planned vs. actual meals, (& caloric intake for each)
- Snacks, alcohol, and other intake
- Upcoming big meals to watch out for

One thing we love: A lot of the tips are designed to help you **break the association** that may exist between **your confidence / happiness** and **your body weight.**

Get yours at <u>habitnest.com/nutrition</u>

Sample Journal Page

◯ **TODAY'S NUTRITION GOAL**

2,100 calories ☑

💧 **WATER DRINKING GOAL**   🚶 **EXERCISE GOAL**

Two 500mL bottles ☑   2 mile jog ☐

🍽 **TODAY'S MEALS**

📅 Planned	✓ Actual	Calories	Protein / Carbs / Fat
3 eggs w/ 2 rice cakes	3 eggs w/ 2 rice cakes	340	18g
Chicken + Broccoli + cauliflower	Burrito (tortilla, avocado, tomatoes, chicken)	800	1.5g
Salmon w/ asparagus	Salmon w/ asparagus	500	51g

🍎 SNACKS, DRINKS, & OTHER

30 almonds	210	9g
One snickerdoodle cookie	250	2.5g
TODAY'S TOTALS:	2,100	82g

🏃 **POTENTIAL FOOD OBSTACLE(S) TO LOOK OUT FOR TOMORROW:**

Resist the cookies at lunch!

⊙ **ONE SMALL WAY I CAN IMPROVE MY NUTRITION TOMORROW IS:**

If I bring a snack to work, I can eat that instead of sweets.

The Weightlifting Gym Buddy
Journal

The Weightlifting Gym Buddy Journal is a complete 12-week personal training program.

No thinking required, just open the journal, follow the workouts, and track your progress. The journal is designed to accompany you to the gym, to help you track your weight/reps for each workout, and to help you compete against yourself every workout.

- **Contains 60 guided workouts for you to follow**

- **Each day's workout targets 2 muscle groups**

- **For lifters of all levels to push themselves to the next level and maximize competition with themselves**

- **Each workout takes 45-60 minutes**

- **Number of reps to aim for is already set for you**

- **Built with a pyramid weight/rep format to intensify each exercise dramatically**

- **No thinking required - just open the journal and follow along for amazing results**

- **Alternative exercises are listed in the case your gym is missing a specific machine**

Get yours at <u>habitnest.com/weightlifting</u>

(You'll see links to exercise guides here each day)

Sample Workout: Biceps & Triceps

DATE _____

1. PREACHER CURL

(ALTERNATIVE: SEATED DUMBBELL CURL)

PREVIOUS BEST	REPS: 5		WEIGHT: 60	

SET 1	REPS: 14	(GOAL: 10-15)	WEIGHT: 40
SET 2	REPS: 10	(GOAL: 8-12)	WEIGHT: 50
SET 3	REPS: 7	(GOAL: 6-8)	WEIGHT: 60
SET 4 (OPTIONAL)	REPS: 6	(GOAL: 4-6)	WEIGHT: 60

2. CLOSE GRIP BENCH PRESS

(By having your "Previous Best" reps and weight values listed for each specific exercise, you'll have a clear target to beat weekly.)

PREVIOUS BEST	REPS: 5		WEIGHT: 50

SET 1	REPS: 13	(GOAL: 10-15)	WEIGHT: 30
SET 2	REPS: 10	(GOAL: 8-12)	WEIGHT: 40
SET 3	REPS: 8	(GOAL: 6-8)	WEIGHT: 50
SET 4 (OPTIONAL)	REPS: 5	(GOAL: 4-6)	WEIGHT: 50

3. ROPE HAMMER CURL

(The fourth set on each exercise is optional but highly recommended.)

PREVIOUS BEST	REPS: 6		WEIGHT: 50

SET 1	REPS: 11	(GOAL: 10-15)	WEIGHT: 35
SET 2	REPS: 11	(GOAL: 8-12)	WEIGHT: 45
SET 3	REPS: 7	(GOAL: 6-8)	WEIGHT: 50
SET 4 (OPTIONAL)	REPS: —	(GOAL: 4-6)	WEIGHT: —

4. OVERHEAD DUMBBELL EXTENSION

PREVIOUS BEST	REPS: 4		WEIGHT: 55

SET 1	REPS: 14	(GOAL: 10-15)	WEIGHT: 35
SET 2	REPS: 12	(GOAL: 8-12)	WEIGHT: 45
SET 3	REPS: 6	(GOAL: 6-8)	WEIGHT: 45
SET 4 (OPTIONAL)	REPS: 5	(GOAL: 4-6)	WEIGHT: 55

TODAY'S WORKOUT INTENSITY: 8.5 / 10

The Badass Body Goals Booty Shaping & Resistance Training

Journal

The Badass Body Goals Booty Shaping & Resistance Training Journal is a full 10-week personal training program which includes 50 guided workouts that are each unique, engaging, and challenging.

The journal is co-written by fitness expert Jennifer Cohen and has a large focus on circuit training (60% of the journal) with a variety of weight training for the remainder.

- The journal is designed to be done at home or in the gym with weights if you want to use more resistance.

- Every journal comes with a timed video guide that allows you to do the workout from beginning to end by simply following along each day.

- Track your results by filling in certain important variables as you complete each workout. As a result, you'll be getting constant encouragement by seeing first-hand how quickly you're improving.

- The journal contains an optimal mix of 4-3-2-1 interval circuits and resistance training workouts workout days. The two are designed to keep you engaged with different movements for short periods which will optimize fat loss and muscle development at the same time.

Get yours at **habitnest.com/badass**

Workout 1: 4-3-2-1

_____
DATE

 30s EACH

GLUTE ACTIVATION WARMUP

a. Clam Opener

(30s Each Leg)

b. Glute Bridge w/ Band Flutter

c. Fire Hydrant

(30s Each Side)

d. Lateral Leg Raise

- 30s Each Leg (w/ Foot Flexed)
- 30s Each Leg (w/ Toes Pointing Down)

——————— 30 SECOND BREAK ———————

60s EACH **CIRCUIT 1**

1a. Curtsy Lunge

REPS: _____
(Left Leg)

→

1b. Curtsy Lunge

REPS: _____
(Right Leg)

→

1c. Boxing Jab

REPS: _____

→

1d. Side to Side Squat

REPS: _____

——————— 30 SECOND BREAK ———————

50s EACH **CIRCUIT 2**

2a. 180° Jump Twist to Floor Tap

SET 1 REPS: _____   →

SET 2 REPS: _____   →

2b. Squat to Overhead Press

SET 1 REPS: _____   →

SET 2 REPS: _____   →

2c. Plie Jump Squat

SET 1 REPS: _____

SET 2 REPS: _____

Bonus Free-Writing Space

213

....
....
....
....
....
....
....
....
....
....
....
....
....
....
....
....
....
....
....
....
....
....
....

....
....
....
....
....
....
....
....
....
....
....
....
....
....
....
....
....
....
....
....
....
....
....
....
....

....
....
....
....
....
....
....
....
....
....
....
....
....
....
....
....
....
....
....
....
....
....
....

....
....
....
....
....
....
....
....
....
....
....
....
....
....
....
....
....
....
....
....
....
....
....
....
....

....

....

....

....

....

....

....

....

....

....

....

....

....

....

....

....

....

....

....

....

....

....

....

....

....

....

....

....

....

....

....

....

....

....

....

....

....

....

....

....

....

....

....

....

Share the Love

If you're reading this, that means you've come pretty far from where you were when starting. You should be extremely proud of yourself!

If you believe this journal has had a positive impact on your life, we invite you to consider gifting a new one to a friend.

Is there a holiday coming up? Is there a special birthday around the corner? Or do you just want to put a smile on someone's face and do something incredible for them?

Gifting this journal is the absolute best way to show any gratitude you may have for what we've written here, as well as serving as a force of good through giving back to others. And you can rest assured that you're helping improve another person's life at the same time.

We created a discount code for getting this far that can be used for any Morning Sidekick Journal reorder (make sure to use the same email address you placed the order with).

If you decide to, feel free to re-order here:
habitnest.com/morning

Use code **MorningChamp15** for 15% off!

Content Index

How Was This Journal Created?

We formulated the journal as a mix between what we find personally effective through our own experience as well as through researching published scientific material and books on the newest, most relevant information we could find.

The following is a mix of studies we used to formulate the journal - some points take ideas found in some sources and mix them with our own experience or with other research points.

Some of the main sources of inspiration came from: Kelly McGonigal's *The Willpower Instinct* (a very science-based book on willpower, it's incredible) and Brian Tracy's *Eat That Frog*.

It is a bit difficult to assign specific studies to specific pages in the book as there is a decent amount of overlap in different sections, though we will do our best.

The 'Why'

Fishbach, Ayelet, and Ravi Dhar. "Goals as Excuses or Guides: The Liberating Effect of Perceived Goal Progress on Choice." Journal of Consumer Research, vol. 32, no. 3, 2005, pp. 370–377., doi:10.1086/497548.

The 'Who'

Clear, James. Atomic Habits. Avery, 2018. pp. 30-34.

Feeling bad makes cake look good: Chun, H., V. M. Patrick, and D. J. MacInnis. "Making Prudent Vs. Impulsive Choices: The Role of Anticipated Shame and Guilt on Consumer Self-Control." Advances in Consumer Research 34 (2007): 715–19.

The what-the-hell effect: Polivy, J., and C. P. Herman. "Dieting and Binging: A Causal Analysis." American Psychologist 40 (1985): 193–201. See also guilt survey: Steenhuis, I. "Guilty or Not? Feelings of Guilt About Food Among College Women." Appetite 52 (2009): 531–34

The 'What'

Gardner, Benjamin, et al. "Making Health Habitual: the Psychology of 'Habit-Formation' and General Practice." *British Journal of General Practice*, vol. 62, no. 605, 2012, pp. 664–666., doi:10.3399/bjgp12x659466.

The 'How'

Tangney, June P., et al. "High Self-Control Predicts Good Adjustment, Less Pathology, Better Grades, and Interpersonal Success." Journal of Personality, vol. 72, no. 2, 2004, pp. 271–324., doi:10.1111/j.0022-3506.2004.00263.x.

Tracking Pages

Fishbach, Ayelet, and Ravi Dhar. "Goals as Excuses or Guides: The Liberating Effect of Perceived Goal Progress on Choice." Journal of Consumer Research, vol. 32, no. 3, 2005, pp. 370–377., doi:10.1086/497548.

Fogg, BJ. "What Causes Behavior Change?" *BJ Fogg's Behavior Model*, www.behaviormodel.org/index.html.

Daily Content

Dieters cheat: Gailliot, M. T., and R. F. Baumeister. "Self-Regulation and Sexual Restraint: Dispositionally and Temporarily Poor Self-Regulatory Abilities Contribute to Failures at Restraining Sexual Behavior." Personality and Social Psychology Bulletin 33 (2007): 173-86.

Distraction and impulsive choices: Shiv, B., and A. Fedorikhin. "Heart and Mind in Conflict: The Interplay of Affect and Cognition in Consumer Decision Making." Journal of Consumer Research 26 (1999): 278–92. See also Shiv, B., and S. M. Nowlis. "The Effect of Distractions While Tasting a Food Sample: The Interplay of Informational and Affective Components in Subsequent Choice." Journal of Consumer Research 31 (2004): 599–608.

Examples of willpower training programs: Baumeister, R. F., M. Gailliot, C. N. DeWall, and M. Oaten. "Self-Regulation and Personality: How Interventions Increase Regulatory Success, and How Depletion Moderates the Effects of Traits on Behavior." Journal of Personality 74 (2006): 1773–801. See also Muraven, M., R. F. Baumeister, and D. M. Tice. "Longitudinal Improvement of Self-Regulation through Practice: Building Self-Control Strength through Repeated Exercise." The Journal of Social Psychology 139 (1999): 446–57.

Progress versus commitment: Fishbach, A., and R. Dhar. "Goals as Excuses or Guides: The Liberating Effect of Perceived Goal Progress on Choice." Journal of Consumer Research 32 (2005): 370–77. See also Fishbach, A., R. Dhar, and Y. Zhang. "Subgoals as Substitutes or Complements: The Role of Goal Accessibility." Journal of Personality and Social Psychology 91 (2006): 232–42.

"Recalling Past Temptations: An Information-Processing Perspective on the Dynamics of Self-Control." Journal of Consumer Research 35 (2008): 586–99.

"Practice the Method." The Wim Hof Method - Become Strong, Happy & Healthy, www.wimhofmethod.com/practice-the-method.

Progress versus commitment: Fishbach, A., and R. Dhar. "Goals as Excuses or Guides: The Liberating Effect of Perceived Goal Progress on Choice." Journal of Consumer Research 32 (2005): 370–77. See also Fishbach, A., R.

Dhar, and Y. Zhang. "Subgoals as Substitutes or Complements: The Role of Goal Accessibility." Journal of Personality and Social Psychology 91 (2006): 232–42.

The brain gets tired: Inzlicht, M. I., and J. N. Gutsell. "Running on Empty: Neural Signals for Self-Control Failure." Psychological Science 18 (2007): 933–37.